CHAMELEON CP PUBLICATIONS

ROCK THE BELLS

AUTHOR OF:
BREAKING THROUGH THE SILENCE

S. Chameleon

Cover Design by: Black Market Logo's
Interior Design: Author S. Chameleon

Special Thank You:

Man, oh man, special thank yous. First off, I'd like to thank God for allowing me to use my gift in a fun and exciting way.

Typically, I don't write long special thank yous, but this time is a little different. It's different because with this novel, I really began to stretch the bar on my creativity and wordplay. I also give you guys an inside look into my sense of humor. By reading Rock the Bells, you're going to get some of everything you've always craved in real life and in real families, but in a book.

First off, let me say that I have a total of eleven sisters and brothers. Six from my father and five from my mother.

With that being said, I am the baby out of six on my mom's side and the third child on my dad's. I grew up with laughter and love all around me.

This novel is in no means a depiction of my family life nor do any of the characters portray any of my siblings, but I just wanted my readers to feel where I am coming from with the story line.

Yes, we as authors do write fiction novels which are technically a literal description of our imagination.

What I want my Chameleon readers to also know is that I am human and go through everyday life as everyone else. I can say that as I created the characters for this awesome Christmas series, I had an absolute blast doing it. Some of them made me sick. Some of them I fell in love with. Some of them I just wanted to choke, and some of them I just wanted to give up to the nearest mission across town.

What I want you all to know is that I wrote this novel for your enjoyment, and if it doesn't keep your interest and keep you laughing, please let a Sista know.

I love all my Chameleon readers, my haters, and my congratulators! Holla at'cha girl…

#Bossup

#Act Like a Lady, Think Like A BOSS!

This book is dedicated to two of the strongest individuals that I've ever known. Even though you're no longer here in body, I feel your spirit every day as I go through life:

My mother

Lois M. Johnson

And

My brother

Richard S. Lewis

May you rest in Heaven and I promise I won't stop!

I will make you both proud!!!

CHAMELEON CP PUBLICATIONS

ROCK THE BELLS

AUTHOR OF:
BREAKING THROUGH THE SILENCE

S. Chameleon

TABLE OF CONTENTS

TABLE OF CONTENTS

CHAMELEON CP PUBLICATIONS

ROCK THE BELLS

AUTHOR OF:
BREAKING THROUGH THE SILENCE

S. Chameleon

PROLOUGE

WHERE IT ALL BEGAN

"This Christmas" by Corinne Bailey Rae played softly in the background. Red, green and orange Christmas lights danced in the distance around the windows.

The whole house was asleep, and Mrs. Regina Bell sat on the couch with her cell phone in hand, waiting to order special sale items on QVC. That was her addiction while her children were down. She used to be a salon owner and beautician but had to retire due to health issues.

Mr. Richard Bell sat at the dinning table eating a homemade cheese Danish and drinking green tea. They watched the clock on the wall waiting for eight a.m. to hit. The anticipation of their five children running down the stairs anticipating opening gift after gift as their little hearts melt with excitement.

The moments slowly slid into seven fifty-four a.m. They listened as little footprints pattered back and forth down the hallway upstairs. The sounds went from their bedrooms to the linen closet to the bathroom.

All freshened up, the kids gathered themselves and filed down to eat breakfast and open gifts.

Mark stood, the oldest of them all. He stepped aside to allow his two younger siblings, Erica and Lance, to hop their way down the stairs. The two were only three years old. Although they were the youngest in the house, their attitude and mannerisms were as if they had been here before.

Sharon and John Carl fought and pushed each other in the background as they waited their turns to go down.

Once they reached the bottom floor, all the children ran straight to the Christmas tree, grabbing gifts and shaking them to see if they would make noise.

"Hold on, children. Not just yet," their mother said. "Everyone to the table for breakfast first, then it'll be time for opening presents."

Erica and Lance went to their seats as did Mark, Sharon and John Carl.

After Mrs. Bell made all the plates, she passed down a short prayer, and they begin to dig in.

Conversation commenced, and after a while, everyone was giving thanks for the things they'd received.

Once nightfall came, so did the extended family. The front door rang back to back as they came in from the cold, leaving chunks of winter on the welcome mat to melt.

There was Mr. Bell's twin brothers Jack and Jackson. They were always the early birds. They'd show up at least two hours before the dinner was done. The two were in their late forties and they were both ladies' men.

Uncle Jack dressed and acted like a drunk foreign exchange student while Uncle Jackson walked around with a bottle of vodka in his right shirt pocket available for immediate sipping with swagged out attire.

Shortly thereafter, Aunt Beattie came hauling in from the church. Aunt Beattie was Mr. Bell's older sister, the oldest of his siblings. She was the no-nonsense type of aunt. She told you how it was and looked you in the eyes when she did. Most of the time, she talked so fast that you could barely understand anything that she said. Just try not to get on her bad side because when she was quiet, that was when she was lethal. She would curse you until the cows came home, and in the same day, bust the doors down at church. At times, she could act bat shit crazy.

Last but not least, you had Aunt Dottie. She was the aunt that had everything. She was cocky, beautiful, and selfish. That was her personality all in a nut shell. She had no children. She had no husband. But she did have a particular set of skills that kept men cashing out on bills and miscellaneous things that she wanted. They knew the arrangements from the gate, and as long as they agreed, she was willing to oblige. Her brothers called it being a hoe, but she always begged to differ.

The holidays were always the times when everyone in the family got together. Outside of the holidays, the adults were always working. The teenagers of the family were in and out of trouble, and the grandparents were in and out of the hospital. But this was the one time of year when you could count on hearing and seeing everyone laughing and partying together.

Once night hit, the liquor was pulled out and so were everyone's true feelings for each other.

THE DAY BEFORE CHRISTMAS EVE
CHAPTER 1

MARRIED BUT SINGLE

Mark stepped out of the shower, dripping wet. He grabbed his bath towel, rubbing his hairy skin until it was all dry. He wrapped a large blue towel around his waist and walked into the walk-in closet to get dressed. As he prepared for his early six a.m. run, he watched his wife as she laid across their bed.

Even though it was almost Christmas they should have been getting on the road to head to his mother's house in Greenville, South Carolina. he really wanted to get his run in. Thinking about it now and looking at his wife's voluptuous curves as she lay lying across their bed, he just may have had a last-minute change of plans.

As he walked into the bedroom, Ashley was reading "Breaking through the Silence" by S. Chameleon on her Kindle. Their son was still asleep.

Mark's deep voice set in as he straddled his wife from behind whispering into her ear, "Baby, you know I love you so much. I would do anything to make you happy."

The smell of the Tom Ford Cologne he'd splashed on his body before leaving the washroom permeated deep into Ashley's nostrils.

As much as she wanted to give in and marvel in his love, the feelings were just not there anymore. She hated to hurt his feelings. She also didn't want to break up their family for lust, but she was in a hard situation and didn't know how to fix it.

Mark hovered over her. His hopes were to turn her on so he could get a little loving before he left the house for his run. Lately, their relationship had just been parent-ship, and it infuriated him to the core.

Father and mother got up in the morning zipping by each other to get ready for work.

Mother dresses and wakes up child. They all leave the house to start their day.

Everyone returned about six or six-thirty p.m.

Mother cook's dinner. Family sits to eat. No conversation given amongst any of them. Just teeth chomping on food and elbows being bent.

Everyone goes their separate ways once their bellies are full. Showers were taken and everyone goes to bed. Same order every day.

Mark and Ashley had stopped having meaningful conversations a while ago.

Mark loved his wife wholeheartedly. He always had Ashley's best interest at heart, and he loved her spirit. She was the mother of his child and he would go to the ends of the earth for his family. Mark just needed to know the magic words or magic move to put on her to make her want him again like she used to.

Ashley, on the other hand, had had mixed feelings for their relationship for about six months and counting. Her shift in feelings wasn't intentional. It kind of just happened.

The feelings she had for Mark just weren't the same anymore. But she vowed to stay through sickness and in health. Now her test had come to pass and Ashley was lying smack dab in the middle of a complicated decision. Trying to block out the feelings she had inside for Randall. He was the maintenance guy at her job. He and Ashely's been banging for a while.

But right now, she still had the issue of her husband trying to get pussy out of her. Should she just ignore the sexual innuendos from her husband at this very moment and make up some sort of excuse?

"Baby, you know you're looking delicious laying across this bed. You know I would really like to make love to you before we leave for vacation," Mark said, almost in a whisper.

Ashley's eyes rolled to the back of her head. She wanted to get up immediately but didn't want to wound her husband's ego.

Mark began winding his hips against her backside. The stiffness of his manhood forewarned Ashley that he was serious and he was trying his all to croon her into having sex with him.

Although she'd blocked him out all together in the last six months, the feeling of his love at that moment felt pleasureful.

The temperature from his breath on the back of her neck made her cookie tingle a little between her legs. She closed her eyes tight and forgot about the what ifs and the hypotheticals for the moment. All she did was focus on the here and now, the soft rubs and caresses from her man. The feeling her right leg began to get when her feelings started to take over their mood was great. The way his breath increased as his member continued to grow underneath his bath towel.

Ashley's breath had soon begun to mimic her husband's in the heat of the moment. She didn't take a second thought. As he lifted his body a little, she turned hers around to face him.

As fast as they could, she pulled at her gown while Mark was yanking at her Victoria's Secret underwear to get them down. Ashley wasn't convinced yet, but what she was about to do was let her husband put the smack down on the P.

Until...

Knock, knock, knock, and a louder knock was delivered to the outside of their bedroom door.

Mark Jr called out for his mother as if his life depended on her helping him with whatever he needed.

"Ma," he continued to call.

Mark Sr put his head down, burying his nose and lips into the side of his wife's neck, blowing hard to get over his annoyance. This was the first time in months he'd even gotten Ashley to move sexually, let alone turn over and entertain the idea of engaging in grown folk activities with him.

In the blink of an eye, his son had taken that moment away from him. This kid knew how to dry up a wet dream, and he was only twelve years old.

"Remind me when we get ready to leave to stuff your son in the trunk for rudely interrupting us," Mark Sr said to Ashley with irritation in his voice.

Ashley displayed a smile across her face as she looked at him getting up from the bed, and it felt nice she thought. Lately she'd been so preoccupied with the idea of busting it open for the maintenance guy that she'd forgotten how caring her husband was.

As much as she wanted to call him back, confess her sins, and jump his bones, she knew that wouldn't happen.

Their son continued to knock.

"Mark Jr., get your paws off my door!" his father yelled, stopping him from knocking.

"Can you ask Mom if she's cooking breakfast before we leave?"

Mark Sr. grabbed the doorknob. He swung the bedroom door open so hard that he could have easily pulled it off the hinges. With every ounce of calmness Mark could muster, he had to steady his breathing while talking to his son, or he would explode.

"Boy, do you know what you..." he said stopping to take a deep breath. "Do you have any flipping idea what the—"

"Wait, wait, wait," Ashley stepped in just before he said too much to their young offspring. "Honey, honey, it's okay. I'm getting up now" Ashley came back with.

"You're getting up? Baby, no. Don't get up. Wait just a second," he continued scrambling around to push their son out. "He can get out," Mark said, pointing at their son as if he had a plague.

"No, baby, I'm going to get up and cook you guys breakfast. It's okay," Ashley continued, rising from the bed and stretching her legs.

"Baby listen, you don't have to get up. Okay look. We don't have to be on the road for another two hours. I say we close our door back and the human that's standing in the doorway right now can go make himself some cereal."

Ashley had to snicker at her husband's desperation to dig into her skin, but she also declined. She stood, shaking her head, not agreeing with her husband's plan.

"Mark, it'll be alright, we have all the time in the world for that," she said, blowing off the importance of their romance.

"No, baby, we don't," Mark Sr whined.

"Look at this kid. I mean, he's practically turning thirty-eight years old soon, and you're about to cook him breakfast? Honey, come on."

"Thirty-eight? Dad, I'm twelve," Mark Jr. said as he looked at his father crazily and his mother as she continued to giggle at her husband's desperate attempt.

"He's not about to be thirty-eight, and yes I'm cooking him a hot meal," Ashley said as she walked into the bathroom to brush her teeth.

Mark Jr. walked out of their room, satisfied that he'd gotten his mother to agree to cook him a hot breakfast. Mark Sr. plopped his disappointed body down on their bed, furious and worried that he'd be developing a serious case of blue balls very soon.

CHAPTER 2

THE SALON OWNER

Sharon was the second oldest. She spent most of her time running her salon Lace Fronts and Lashes. Also, caring for her small children while her fiancé worked as a factory worker and boss. Sharon had owned her shop now for six years.

She and her better half, Gerald, had been together for five years. They had made five years about six weeks ago.

Although Sharon was in love with him and happy that they even made it to five years, she had some insecurity about their relationship.

Sharon had always been a beautiful redbone, offering everything physically that a man would want. There was just one little problem. Gerald had managed to crumble her heart, making her vulnerable in the same five years that they were supposed to be growing and building together.

He not only had gotten caught cheating before, but he was supposed to have a baby on the way. Sharon wanted so badly to kill him and just walk away from the relationship, but she just couldn't.

When he was home, he was good to her. When he wanted to be charming, he always was. Finally, he was a down right beast in the sheets.

If he wasn't flipping Sharon upside-down, he was making her ride his curve. From there it was as if he'd turned into a beast like Kevin Gates nasty ass. He'd go from flipping her over to licking her ass then sloppily eating her pussy. That would quickly go to him bending her over, coaching her face downtown to pleasure him with her mouthpiece. Her body always gave in.

She loved Gerald just that much. All those years they'd grown together, to throw it all away for momentary weakness. That was all that continued to play over and over in her head.

Sharon met Gerald about a week after her high school graduation, which was now coming close to being ten years ago, at first, they were just friends. After a few years, they became more.

If you asked them both together how was life, you'd get all the smiles, bells, and the whistles in the response, but behind closed doors, Gerald and Sharon went at it day in and day out. It was like living with vicious animals twenty-four hours a day.

Sharon always felt if she stuck around and stuck by Gerald's side, they'd get the old them back. Maybe he'd begin to be more supportive for the things that she wanted to accomplish. She wanted to take her business on the road. She wanted to enter big hair battles. She wanted to give seminars teaching people proper etiquette to care for their hair. She had big dreams for Lace Fronts and Lashes.

Gerald couldn't care less about all that. He knew he was up for a promotion at his job. If Sharon started to travel and go on the road, he'd be left home with the kids. There was no way in hell he was going to miss work because she wanted to be a traveling bag of weave bundles.

While he continued to ignore the woman that he loved, she sat in the wings waiting for the big moment for Gerald to wake up a realize that she would not always be there to pick up the pieces.

****

"Sharon!" Gerald yelled from the bottom of the stairs. "Woman, I know you hear me calling you. Are you ready?"

Sharon came walking down the stairs with six inch heels on, carrying their eight-month old baby on her hip.

Her lips popped with "Wet Dreams" gloss complements of Chameleon Cosmetics. A new cosmetics line that she's featuring in her shop. Her breasts peeked out of her white tank covered in Vicki's. Gerald gawked at the fine specimen that came towards him almost about to drool if he didn't know any better.

Sharon stopped in her tracks directly in front of Drooling Drake standing in front of her.

"Gerald, what is wrong with you? Why stand there looking stupid?" she asked, walking by him, pushing his shoulder to move him out of her path.

"Sharon, why do you have to dress so provocative? We're only going to a family holiday weekend, not a Slippery Thot convention."

"Slippery!" Sharon popped back. "Thot! Okay, Gerald, I got your slippery thot. You always sliding some slick ass shit out your mouth. When I leave your ass for being disrespectful, we gone see who gone be a thirsty thot then," she told him while putting their baby in the car seat so they could leave. She grabbed the car keys from the sofa table and yelled for their daughter Cammy to come on so they could go.

She turned quickly, lifting the car seat, propping it on her left arm.

"Get the bags and bring 'em to the car," she said before turning to walk out the door, then doubling back.

"Oh, and by the way, I wasn't too much of a thot when you popped two babies up in me," she said, pointing at her own vagina.

"Man, if you don't shut up. You always running your mouth," Gerald said, trying to stand up for himself, grabbing the first bag with force while swooping up the others in his arm as he was told.

He walked them to the car and neatly set them in the trunk for their trip across town to his in-laws. They all stayed over for the whole weekend. If they took their bags with them, they wouldn't have to come back to their house for anything.

Gerald glided into the driver's seat. He turned to make sure the kids were all buckled in in the back seat before starting the SUV.

"Don't worry, I buckled them in, stupid. It's your seatbelt you need to check. I wouldn't want you to fly your ass out the windshield in case of a crash," Sharon said before snapping her own belt for security and rolling her eyes at Gerald.

Gerald sat back uncomfortably in his seat and checked his belt once, twice, then a third time before backing out of the driveway.

Sharon and Gerald, little Cammy, and baby Poodah were all ready and on the road heading to Sharon's parents to spend time with them and her siblings.

Gerald just hoped that they could keep it together for the weekend while they were there. Dealing with Sharon, that would always be an iffy situation.

CHAPTER 3

THE ESCORT

John Carl! The infamous John Carl Bell. What do you not say about the ladies' man? He stood six feet two inches tall. Dark complected with more of a perfect nose than Brad Pitt. The dimples in his cheeks were just an added bonus for all his ladies.

John Carl was an aspiring realtor, but in the meantime, he lived off his prospects. His women. His special friends.

Asking any of the women who they were to him would set off a shit storm. Each of them thought they were the main catch, but none of them ever were.

John Carl would always let it be known to the woman, and their men if they wanted to know. To maintain a relationship with him, they would have to sign a contract to keep him on retainer for the duration of the written obligation. Anything he spent in access would be invoiced out to them later.

He needed just a little bit more dough in his stash to pay for the full cost of his realtor's exam. He'd finished all the necessary classes. He just didn't like the idea of using his own money when there were so many other willing individuals looking to donate to his cause.

If it wasn't one thing, it was another with John Carl. Either he was entertaining company or hosting someone else's event with his witty charm and debonair sex appeal.

He never kept a woman. To be honest, he didn't want to keep a woman. He was the tender age of thirty. He felt there was no need for commitment. There were so many women in the world that just wanted a night away every now and again. He seemed to be a magnet for those types of creatures. As soon as John Carl ran into a prospective trap, he was on it like heat rash.

****

John Carl got up from his bed and headed straight for the bathroom. He turned on the hot water in the sink for it to warm while he stood waiting to take a wiz in the toilet.

"Hmmm… Today's going to be a good day," he said to himself as he admired his good looks in the mirror.

John Carl lived in Greenville, South Carolina along with his parents. He was that one grown child who still lived at home. As high strung as he was, it never seemed to bother him that he demanded things from others but at the same time didn't have any real responsibilities.

John Carl brushed his teeth and covered his face with Noxzema. He jumped in the shower to get fresh. He needed to run some errands before his siblings started to pull in.

He ran by the cleaners to pick up some clothes that he needed and ran into an old friend from back in high school, Amanda Teech.

Amanda was the head cheerleader in school and never gave John Carl the time of day. She had to do a double take as she saw a man that she thought looked familiar to her. Instead of just staring, she decided to talk to him to see if they knew each other.

"Excuse me, but do we know each other?"

John Carl turned, looking down at her. The way they locked eyes, you'd swear they'd fallen in love at first sight.

"I'm sorry I don't believe we do. I'd remember knowing such a beautiful woman as you" He lied.

"Oh, and you're charming, too. My name is Amanda," she said, holding out her hand for him to shake. "Amanda Teech, and you are?"

"John Carl. John Carl Bell. It's a pleasure meeting you."

Amanda displayed the biggest smile while holding her grasp on his hand.

"John Carl Bell, I knew I had seen your face before. You and I went to the same high school. You went to Mauldin, right?"

"Yeah, I did," he said, still trying to recall just who she was from school.

"I was the cheerleading captain the whole time we were in school."

"Oh, okay, okay. Amanda..." he dragged out her name and motioned at the front of his chest as if he were bouncing large breasts.

"Well, if that's the way you'll remember me, then yes. Amanda..." she sang back, but this time bouncing her own large breasts right in front of him.

John Carl had to laugh at his identifier for her. Not meaning to offend her but making sure she was who he thought she was. They stood and had small talk while their orders were being prepared.

"So, John Carl, what are you doing with yourself these days? I know most of the people we graduated with are all married or dead," Amanda said, and they both laughed.

"Actually, I'm studying to be a realtor. But in the meantime, I'm working as a male escort."

Amanda nearly severed the tip of her tongue as she chewed her gum while getting stumped on John Carl's last comment.

He walked closer to her and patted her on the back. "Are you okay?"

"Uh, yes. I'm fine, I'm fine. I just didn't expect for you to say that you were a male escort."

John Carl reached over the counter for his clothes and threw them over his left arm.

"What do you mean, you didn't expect me to say that? What did you expect for me to say? That I was a banker? Or a factory worker?" he asked while licking his full lips.

"Wow, I've never known a real life male prostitute before."

"Well, that could be because I'm not a prostitute. I prefer male servant. If the price is right, I can wine and dine you. When your tab is running, the sky is the limit. Normally, I don't have sexual intercourse with my clients," he expressed while hanging his clothes up in his back seat of his car.

As soon as he shut the back door, Amanda moved in just a little closer. The interest in her eyes was oozing out.

Amanda leaned against John Carl's car and folded her arms comfortably.

"So, John Carl, what do you do about relationships? Do you have children?"

"Don't need one and no. Listen, I'm young. I don't have time for a relationship, and children equal shit diapers. Not my style."

Amanda let out a quick smirk as she stood tall to her feet.

"So, Amanda, I can tell by the smirk on your face that you're not buying the whole escort thing, are you?"

"I mean, it's your story. I just don't see how you get desperate woman to pay you for your company," she said, shaking her head and digging into her bag for her car keys.

"You have to understand, it's not always about someone being desperate. For example, I have a client that pays my agency two hundred and fifty dollars for me to meet her at a hotel every other Saturday at two in the morning. She's married, beautiful, and comfortable with her spouse. She just craves more, and I give her that. After she showers, we lie in bed naked while I rub her down with warm oil. The remainder of my time is spent giving her brain the wettest orgasm she has ever had."

Amanda had to take a deep breath and clear her throat to make sure she heard him correctly.

"So, you're telling me for two hundred and fifty dollars you'd get me in a dark room, rub me down with warm scented oil, and whisper nasty things in my ear in hopes that it will make me climax?"

John Carl looked down at her left hand and spotted a large single rock on her hand. Had to be a minimum of four karats. She's a gold mine, he thought.

Slowly, he slid in her direction. Amanda's heart was about to burst out of her chest. She could feel her pearl begin to pulsate.

His breath was warm on her neck. It felt like her baby hairs were being fanned quickly. Amanda was lost in the moment.

Intrigued with John Carl's conversation, looks, and abilities, without paying attention, she'd been backed against the back door of his car again.

John Carl bent down to her left ear, his breaths were steady, and his body language was consistent with sex. He could feel the intense heat between himself and Amanda. He just wanted to make her a believer.

"Amanda, I thought it was cute how you added your own twist to the evening with scented oil. I promise you whichever oil I use, you would appreciate it." He continued through laborious breath, "I'd rub every inch of your body slow. Applying pressure on the spots that make you glide like a snake," he expressed.

He took a short but deliberate breath directly in her ear. He needed her to feel what he felt.

"I'd tie your hands and feet with silk only as a bonus to make you yearn for that special feeling. Slowly, I'd tease the tip of your clit with my special feather teaser."

He released another torn breath.

"I'd play with your nipples. I'd make you want so much more. I'd tease every inch of your body. Licking your pearl wet then sucking it dry and drenching it again. I'd make your cookie make noises you never imagined that it could. I will make the feeling take over you."

The more intense John Carl got with the explanation of his career, the more Amanda started to feel a twinkle of juices from her palace.

"Mmmm... Amanda," he whispered while lightly licking the tip of her ear.

"Yes?" she answered with her eyes closed and her lips puckered for a kiss.

John Carl stood to his feet and walked away.

When she heard feet moving, she opened her eyes and John Carl was standing at the driver's door of his car, holding it open.

"I know that look, Amanda," he said to her over the top of the car. "Be careful what you wish for. I'm going to act like I didn't just see you get all hot and bothered."

Amanda still stood in the same spot against John Carl's car. Moist, horny, and cotton mouthed. She had no idea what to do first. She'd dropped her clothes on the ground. So first, she'd start by picking them up.

She had no words, but she did have a whole picture in her mind of what she would do with John Carl if she ever had the chance.

A girl can wish, right? Hell, I'm engaged. not dead, she thought.

As John Carl drove off, Amanda stood on the sidewalk watching as his tail lights got further and further away.

John Carl drove alone, thinking to himself that he may have just won the jackpot with old Amanda Teech. He'd give her about a week, then he'd call her and ask her out for lunch. Not to seduce her. Just lunch.

CHAPTER 4

THE TWINS

Lance was where things began to get a little bit complicated with the Bell family. Mrs. Bell had delivered not one, but two little bundles of joy. The first by two minutes was Lance. The Momma's boy. Lance had always been his own person. A little peculiar, some would think by his style. But all in all, Lance was a straight up person. Not your everyday socialite, but he could learn to grow on you.

Lance and his twin, Erika, they were identical. Identical in looks but not in life. Lance had been in a relationship with his partner for two years. David was his name. He loved Lance to death. If he could calm him down a little, he would, but outside of that, they seemed to be just as happy as anyone else.

Lance's flamboyant tendencies came out by the day the older he got. When he was younger, he had to hide who he was for his parents' sake. Once he came out to his family and began to feel comfortable with himself, he embraced who he really was.

You'd swear you were in the room with the head Queen. He'd honey, baby, and boo-boo you through a full conversation. Once Lance started going by the name of LaLa, the family eventually got tired of fighting. They just dealt with what he expressed to them was his happiness.

Most of the siblings understood his position and gave him their blessing. All except for Mark. He hated the fact that his brother chose to be in the world as he called it.

Lance tried having conversations with his brother to try to get him to understand his position. Mark wouldn't hear of it.

After trying and trying and trying, Lance gave up. He continued to enjoy his life as being an openly gay man.

In the meantime, whenever Mark was in his presence, he cringed at the sight of seeing his brother pop his ass harder than a stripper.

Erika, was totally opposite her counterpart. She was the sweetest. She was so quiet all the time, she'd have you wondering if she even knew how to speak. The only person in the family that could get her to talk or interact with the rest of the family was Lance. If he was around, you could bet a pretty penny you'd see Erika close by, smiling.

A twenty-five-year-old virgin. A science wiz. Accepted to four of the most prestigious colleges in the country.

None of that meant anything to Erika. Every single application, she turned down. She stayed home right in her comfort zone with her brother, Lance, who she now shared an apartment with.

Lance had been thinking hard lately of moving out on his own, but as it seemed he was in a hasty attempt to spare his twin's feelings.

****

"Awww, shit. Girl, if you don't get down those stairs. You better," Lance cheered to his sister Erika. She walked down the stairs with her legs closed tight at the knees.

Lance had convinced her to step all the way out of her element. He picked her clothes to wear for the weekend. She had on a pair of black leggings and an oversized off the shoulder sweater accented by a pair of black wedge heels that she had no idea how to walk in.

As she hit the bottom step, she tripped a little trying to do a model twirl for her brother.

If Erika were ever in a bad mood, Lance would be the one to pull her out of her funk.

The new haircut she had gotten became her. She stood in the bathroom for an hour just looking at it and making faces. Give her a white handkerchief or a baseball cap, and she normally would be good with her hair.

As her brother made a big deal about how she looked, her geek tendencies were beginning to kick in. She'd spaced out for a moment thinking of what her next read would be. She could easily read four or five books in a week's time.

You could even catch her talking politics to the television. That was about the most you would get out of sweet Erika. I guess we would have to see what this holiday will bring for everyone.

CHAPTER 5

ALMOST CHRISTMAS

Regina stood in the kitchen sipping on her tea slowly looking out the kitchen window as her children began to arrive. Lance and Erika were already there. They had come over early this morning to do their mother's last minute store runs.

"Hey, Momma! Give me a hug, beautiful. I've missed you so much," Mark expressed, hugging his mother and lifting her from the ground.

"Put me down, boy. You really got to be excited to see me then, huh," she laughed, hitting his shoulder as he put her down.

"Hello, Mother," Ashley spoke, walking up to hug her mother-in-law.

"Hey, baby. How you doing? You haven't called me lately. What's the matter? That son of mine working on your nerves?"

"No, Mother, I'm so sorry about that. I've just been very preoccupied with work is all."

"Yeah, a little too preoccupied, Mother," Mark commented.

"Don't start this early, Mark," Ashley commented back crudely.

"Mother, don't pay him any mind. He's going through some sort of midlife crisis."

Regina and Ashley laughed off the awkward moment while Mark and Mark Jr. brought the bags in out of the car. Just as they were grabbing the last of the bags, Sharon, Gerald, and their children were pulling up.

"Pull over there, Gerald. If you park right here, no one else will be able to park here."

"Sharon, let me handle the driving. You've dictated every inch of the road on the way here. At least let me choose where and how to park the car, will you please?" Gerald asked sarcastically.

"Don't be a smart-ass, Gerald. And the last time I checked, when you followed your own mind, you slipped into some ratchet pussy and got a girl pregnant, so we'll go with my choice for three hundred, Alex."

Gerald looked over at Sharon, shaking his head. She got on his nerves in more ways than one, but he loved her to death and she did take him back after he got caught cheating, so he could understand her point a little. He just had to remind himself of that every day in order to hold himself back from strangling her.

Once they parked the car, Sharon jumped out and hugged her nephew, Mark Jr., and smacked her brother, Mark Sr., on the back of the head.

"What's going on, chump? You ready to get beat in a family game of tunk? I hope you brought your quarters," Sharon threatened her older brother.

"Sis, please, you know I got my money. You just make sure your fiancé didn't leave y'all money at home in your sock drawer."

They all laughed because not only did everyone in the family know that Sharon had Gerald's balls in a vice grip right now, but he couldn't seem to make a conscious decision lately to save his life. Sharon had been on his ass like white on rice. Since the last incident of him being caught cheating, she'd been on him like a heat rash, and he if he knew what was best, he'd straighten up before Sharon decided to let his ass off at the next stop.

"Aww, bro, that's how you gone do me?" Gerald asked through his own laugh as he helped Sharon get the kids out of the car.

When they got in the house, commotion was coming almost from all the rooms in the house. Regina stood in the kitchen making small talk with Sharon and Erika.

Gerald and Mark stood in the backyard over a deep fryer talking with Mr. Bell. Collectively, they were trying to figure out the best strategy for Mr. Bell to deep fry their first turkey.

"Dad, you think this is a good idea? Why don't we just pay somebody to deep fry this thing?" Mark offered up to his father.

"Boy, that's the problem with this here generation. Y'all lazy as all get out. When you want, something done right, you do it yourself. Save your coins. Don't be out here paying all these made-up chefs to cook the major part of your holiday dinner. I got this all under control," Mr. Bell said, holding an oven mitt in one hand and a large fork for poking in the other.

"Dad, that's right. You show these boys how real men do it for the holidays," Sharon offered up as she walked out into the backyard from the house.

"Hey, baby girl!" Mr. Bell called out as he saw his daughter's face. "Dad's so happy to see his little peach pie. How you been, baby?"

"I've been okay, Daddy. I could be even better if I could find a man like you, Daddy."

"Oh, honey. Don't say that. I like my future son-in-law," he said, looking over at Gerald, who was trying to purposely ignore their conversation.

"Yeah, well you don't have to live with him, Daddy."

"And your daddy hasn't lived with you since you were eighteen years old, so make sure you tell the whole story, Miss Sharon Latriece Bell," Gerald said, butting in.

"Shut up, Gerald. Nobody's talking to you."

"Come on, kids," Mr. Bell called out.

"We're all going to have a stress-free weekend. No arguing," Mr. Bell let them know, so they wouldn't have any other misunderstandings.

Just as they got that issue cleared up, another ensued in minutes. Their holiday weekend had just started, and attitudes had begun to fly already.

Lance came walking around the house from the front yard. He'd just pulled up from picking up David from work. They stopped by to say hi before going home for David to shower.

The look on Mark's face was as if his nose was full of a shitty smell. He wanted to see his brother, but he could pass on David, and he let that be known.

"Hey, Lance, how you doing, little brother?" Mark said with a sarcastic tone.

"How are you, Marcus?" Lance said back before smacking his lips and rolling his eyes at his brother.

"You gotta do all that when you say hi? A man would just say hello and keep it moving."

"So, if that's the case, then what's your damn problem?" Lance asked while stopping in his brother's face, squeezing all his fingers together in front of his face.

Mark walked past David, shaking his head in disgust.

"Hello, Mark," David spoke.

Mark kept walking and didn't part his lips to speak back.

"Daddy, you better tell your son we not gone deal with the rudeness this weekend. David is not going anywhere, so he needs to just get over it."

"When fat ass pigs fly," Mark said aloud for everyone to hear.

"Hey! Listen you two. Ain't no damn pigs gone fly around my house, and ain't nobody gone be rude. Get it together before everyone gets here. Now kiss and make up. Now!" he exclaimed.

Lance walked over to Mark putting out his arms for his brother to embrace him in a loving hug.

Once their arms were linked, Lance whispered in his brother's ear, "I know you hate my gay ass and my gay ass boyfriend, but if you keep acting that way, I'll have to just hold you down and lick your face," he said through a light laugh.

"And that will be your first time being shot," Mark said back jokingly to his little brother.

"It's good to see you two smiling now," David said.

Mark turned to look back at him. He shook his head and walked into the house to get out of the lion's den.

As he walked into the kitchen, he stuck his finger in the bowl his mother was mixing cake batter in.

"Boy, get back," Mrs. Bell said, smacking his hand back from her cake batter.

After sticking his finger in his mouth then wiping with a paper towel, Mark laughed then went out to stand on the front porch to smoke a cigarette.

John Carl was backing his E Class in the driveway just as he walked out.

"Look at this pretty boy," Mark spoke about his brother as he walked up.

"What's going on, brother? How's it going? Glad you and your family could make it."

"I know, man," he said, shaking his brother's hand, giving the half-hug greeting.

"I see you still riding around here in the latest," he said, referring to John Carl's new ride.

"Yeah, man. You know how it is. My ladies like to see me in the finest things. That right there was just a little bonus for my loyalty."

"Well, I wonder what you'd get once you get her to bust it open."

John Carl and Mark had to laugh at Mark's last statement. Mark was as stiff as a board, and to hear him say somebody was busting it open was just not right.

"Bro, don't ever let anybody hear you say somebody was busting nothing open. That phrase is so off limits to you."

The two had to laugh because as hard as Mark tried to stay up to date not to be left out of the loop to be cool, it just wasn't part of his character.

"Look, I ain't as bad as you try to make me seem," Mark said, trying to defend himself.

"Bro, listen, you almost old as Jesus, and you gone sit up here and tell me Ashley still be busting it open for you?"

Mark stood to the side, staring at the top of the tree in their parents' front yard. With no answer, five seconds later, Mark and John Carl burst into laughter.

Both of them knew through all the shit that Mark would talk around the family, he wasn't getting sex, head, or attention at home.

That was what made the whole bust it open situation even more funny.

Gerald walked out onto the front porch to join his soon to be brothers-in-law.

"What y'all got going on out here?" he asked while giving John Carl some dap.

"We out here talking about how Mark here aint getting no cookies out the cookie jar."

"Oh damn, bro. Your wife aint giving you no pussy?" Gerald yelled out as if it were a crime.

As he lit his cigarette, he walked down off the porch steps from by the door.

"Man, it ain't no way I'm about to be living with my woman and I ain't hitting the skins. I mean, man, come on. We as men are entitled to unlimited punnai," he continued to say, giving his opinion.

What he didn't know was that Sharon had come out of the house and was standing right behind him listening to every word he dropped with confidence.

"Listen, bro. Your sister and I, we have our issues. But when it comes to sex, I can't be denied that. That shit keeps me going," he continued to say, dragging on his cigarette.

"Oh, is that right?" Sharon asked from behind his head. She was so close, he could feel the heat from her breath. Abruptly, he jumped, almost falling off the porch step he was standing on.

"Woman! Don't be rolling up on me like that. I keep trying to tell you," he said as John Carl and Mark laughed their asses off at the frightened look on his face.

"Gerald, you better stop standing out here lying to these people. We have the same parents. They can smell bullshit from miles away," Sharon said, shutting her husband down once again.

"Damn, she just punked yo ass out politely, nigga. You ain't gone get your lick back?" John Carl joked as he and Mark laughed at the dumb look on Gerald's face.

Gerald looked over at the two and shook his head. He headed back up the stairs to go into the house. "You two need some serious medication."

"And you need a divorce attorney, but we can't all get what we want, can we?"

The laughter that came from them all even made Gerald laugh, and he was the one being cracked on.

Sharon, Mark, and John Carl followed Gerald into the house. They all walked into the sitting room. Their mother had prepared homemade Christmas cookies that sat on trays atop each table. Soft tunes of Anita Baker's Christmas Fantasy played in the background, and everyone got comfortable.

Lance and Erika came walking down the stairs and headed into the sitting room to join everyone else.

"Oh Lord, here come Little Richard and Debbie Allen," Mark said sarcastically referring to Lance and Erika.

"Mark, I heard what you said. Now, you can just go play in traffic for me, please," he said throwing his hand up in his brother's face.

"I'll go play in traffic if you're holding my hand, Lolita."

Lance's balled fists and puffed jaws showed everyone in the room that he'd had enough of Mark's shit already. They hadn't even gotten to the family's first event, and they were already about to kill each other.

"Hey, hey, hey my, babies," Mrs. Bell said, walking into the room, wiping her hands on the bottom of her apron. "What y'all got going on in here?" she asked, breaking up the tension in the air.

Lance's eyes were still planted right on Mark. He wanted to rip his ribs through his throat so badly. Just for the few seconds Mark made eye contact with Lance.

Lance was sure to mouth enough for a threat.

"Yo momma just saved yo life," he whispered in the air at Mark as he smiled a little and put his attention back on their mother.

"Listen, everybody. Since everyone is here, I want to have each of you put your name on one of these little pieces of paper. Put it in this here mixing bowl," she said, setting it in the middle of the living room table.

Each of them did as they were told and put their names on the paper folded and back in the mixing bowl.

When their mother came back, she had Aunt Beattie with her. She needed that extra person to pull the names out.

"Okay, everybody. We are about to pull names for Christmas gifts. No re-gifting and no overspending. The spending limit is twenty dollars for adults and ten dollars for kids."

Between breaths, Mark started to cough while raising his hand at the same time.

"What, Marcus?" Mrs. Bell asked, being funny by calling him by his government name.

"Momma, the spending limit twenty dollars, is that right?"

"Yes, Marcus, why?"

"Oh, I was just asking 'cause if I get Sharon, and I want to buy her a coat, I'ma have to buy a feather down comforter to cover that big ass back of hers and that's going to exceed the monetary limit."

Everyone in the room almost died from laughing at Mark's sarcasm.

"Listen, I'm not trying to be funny," he said.

"Yes, you are, you monkey dog. Momma, you better get your child," Sharon said. "I hope you choke on your toothbrush in the morning, you spider monkey," Sharon shot back.

"Guess I better not brush my teeth in the morning then, huh? I wouldn't want Mrs. Baby Hannibal over there putting a hex on my brush bristles."

Mark had taken that joke just a little bit too far, and now everyone was looking at him with the "bruh man" stare.

"Okay, sorry, that was a little much, wasn't it?" Mark asked, and everyone laughed again including their mother.

These fun times were what they lived for. Family was everything. Even through all the arguing, the fussing and the fighting, they still reigned victorious in the loving and compassion department. With tomorrow being Christmas Eve, everyone prepared for bed early. They had a long family day of shopping to prepare for that was going to begin at five a.m.

CHAPTER 6

ROUND # 1 FAMILY SHOPPING

Five a.m. alarms were sounding off in everyone's room. Mark jumped up, shaking his wife for her to get up and get their son together.

While Sharon was in their room doing the same and getting her and Gerald's kids together, Mrs. Bell and Mr. Bell sat at their bedsides drinking coffee, listening to all the commotion out in the hallway. Their kids were yelling and scrambling, trying to get everyone together for their morning of shopping together.

It had always been family tradition for them all to pull names and get together the next morning to shop.

The whole family piled up in a van that Mr. Bell rented just for this occasion. He wanted it to be enough room so that no one would be left behind or go off anywhere else.

Once they got to Haywood Mall, everyone made sure their cells were charged. All the babies were with their parents and Mr. and Mrs. Bell found the first cushy leather massage chairs in the middle of the mall that they could find.

Mr. Bell already knew he was only going to shop in one store. The "Made for TV" store. He didn't care if he had a child or an adult, he'd find something for everyone in that store.

Mrs. Bell had had her gift for the last six months. All her money was spent ordering unnecessary shit from QVC day in and day out. She'd been ordering from them since her children were young. If you asked her what she wanted for her birthday, she would ask for a Visa gift card so she could use it to order something she didn't need from QVC. She had so much mess in their garage that she had enough unisex gifts to last her for five Christmases.

"Honey, these kids gone be shopping for about four hours," Mrs. Bell said to Mr. Bell as they got comfortable in their massage chairs.

"I know it, Regina, but that's what we're here for. We do this every year and you have the same complaint, honey. As soon as they're all done shopping, we will head back home for you to get back into the television to order another trinket from QVC," he assured her.

Although Mrs. Bell loved to have her family all together, she hated when it involved her missing a product that QVC was doing a special on.

After hearing her husband's response, she sat back in her seat and relaxed out her wait.

One hallway down, Sharon and Gerald were arguing about who was going to pay the five dollars for the mall's baby stroller.

"I ain't got no money. Your ass always trying to use the last of what I got," Gerald argued with Sharon.

"Gerald, I'm not about to go through this shit with you today. Give me the five dollars or hand over the keys to my car."

Gerald wiped over his face, releasing the sweat that had built up from his frustration.

"Oh my God, woman. I have never in my life known a person that was so selfish. You will suck the life out of a nigga, I swear," he said, handing over the five dollars as she had requested.

Sharon stuck the money in the machine, stuffed her purse and jacket in the back, and buckled the baby in. They were off, dipping in this store and dipping in that store, arguing with each other one minute and kissing the next. They stood at the jewelry counter looking at watches for Mrs. Bell. That was who Sharon had picked. She'd planned to buy her mother a really pretty watch. If she could catch one on sale, she just may have been able to get her a bracelet too. She just didn't want to go over the twenty-dollar limit.

As the store attendant walked up, Sharon noticed how Gerald had begun to fidget around like he had to use the bathroom.

"Hello, ma'am, my name is Rebecca. Is there anything I can help you with?" the store attendant asked. When Sharon looked up, standing in front of her was a beautiful chocolate woman. Her skin was so clear, Sharon could tell she didn't have on a bit of makeup. Her hair flowed at least fifteen inches from her neck. It looked as if she'd had it blown out. For a moment, she just stood there looking at her without saying a word.

"Ma'am?" the lady said again. "Ma'am, is there anything I can help you with?"

"Oh, shit, yeah," Sharon said, breaking herself from her trance. "I wanted to look at a couple of these watches as a gift for my mother. Would you happen to have any that are on sale?"

"Yes, ma'am, we do. Our sale watches are right over here in this case," she said, pointing just over to the side.

As they walked over, Gerald stayed standing in the same spot, looking around at the bracelets on a rounder as if he were interested in them.

"G, come on. We're going over here," Sharon told her boo so he'd stay close by them.

The sales attendant looked up, noticing Gerald was a face that she hadn't seen in a while. She looked at Sharon, and she had on a wedding ring, but when she looked over at Gerald, he didn't, so she figured maybe they were just family members.

Assuming the coast was clear, she cut into Gerald, not knowing that Sharon was his fiancée, and she was half out of her mind.

Rebecca pulled out three watches and handed them over to Sharon. She wanted to give her time to look them over and choose which she liked best. She walked away from Sharon just for a second to tend to her suspicion.

"Excuse me," she spoke loudly in Gerald's direction.

Sharon's ears immediately popped open like eye spy. "Sir, excuse me."

Gerald looked up and turned around slowly. He didn't want to turn into a right hand from his baby momma.

"I thought that was you," Rebecca said with a huge smile.

"Gerald, it's me, Rebecca. I know you remember who I am, don't you?"

Gerald shook his head no then yes. Then he looked over at his fiancée's face and exhaled as if it would be his last breath.

"Nah, I'on think we know each other," he said.

"Oh, come on, Gerald. I know it's been about six months, but I know you remember who I am. Remember at the club on Congaree Road? Rebecca with the good Becky. You're telling me you've forgotten all that?" she continued to ask.

When she let out that last statement, Gerald felt like slitting his own wrist.

"Gerald, so who is Rebecca with the good Becky? What the hell is that supposed to mean?" Sharon asked, turning all the way around, snapping her hands onto the handle of the baby stroller she was pushing. She pushed it over to the side, waiting for an answer.

"Somebody gone answer my mother flipping question or we gone get some slaps going on up in here," she threatened.

"Sharon, I don't know this woman. I have no idea what she's talking about. Maybe she has me mixed up with somebody else," he said, trying not to make eye contact with Rebecca.

"So, Rebecca with the good head, now I'll ask you because I know this nigga lying. How do you know my fiancée?"

"Fiancée?" she repeated. "I'm sorry, I didn't know he was he was engaged to be married. I met him at a club. A friend of mine introduced us. We slept together two or three times. After the last time, I never heard from him again," she said.

Everything Rebecca knew, she was letting out. She didn't want to be in the middle of anybody's baby momma drama.

"So, Gerald, you sliding up on thot ass store clerks now, huh?"

Gerald looked over at Sharon and decided to just keep his mouth shut. Anything he tried to come out his mouth with at this point wouldn't make a bit of a difference.

"Rebecca, since my careless ass man forgot to include you in all of the details of his life, here it is," Sharon said, smacking her lips, getting ready to release a mouthful.

"Gerald here is engaged and and has been for five years. He has two wonderful children who he adores but don't respect. He also has me who has tried to stand by his cheating ass over and over and over again. He also has a me that's going to put his ass out when they get back home until he can get his shit together," she continued, rolling her eyes. "And lastly, he also has a fiancée that will snap your frail neck if you ever in your life think about sleeping with him again."

Sharon slid her arm across the jewelry counter, wiping everything out that was set atop it. There were watches, bracelets, and pendants hitting the floor faster than Rebecca could grab.

"Gerald, you ain't gone be satisfied until me and my kids are gone. You gone keep playing with my emotions, and you gone find yourself alone. I promise you that," Sharon said as tears began to gather in the corner of her eyes.

"Sharon, please, baby, listen," he said, trying to get her to turn and face him. "Baby, please let me talk to you. Can we just sit down and talk about this?"

"Gerald, I'm sick of talking. I've talked to you until I was blue in the face. I am not a bad woman, and before I let you run my esteem into the ground, I will leave your sorry ass."

"No, baby, no," he said, grabbing her arm.

"Sharon, please listen to me. That was a long time ago, baby" He hurried to get out

"I thought you didn't know who she was? Lying muthafucka"

"Okay, I don't. But listen," he said, fumbling around with his words.

"See, Gerald, you can't even be honest with me after all I just said to you."

Sharon turned and walked away. Pushing their baby in the stroller while allowing Cammy to hold on to the side so they could stay together.

Gerald stood still in the same spot, completely taken aback by what had just happened. He couldn't have predicted this shit even if he wanted to.

He knew Sharon was livid. The ride home with her was going to be pure hell. Gerald had made his bed, and it was beginning to haunt him before he ever got a chance to even lie in it. He just hoped this instance would be the first and only this weekend. He didn't think he and Sharon's relationship could take any more hiccups or surprises.

CHAPTER 7

ROUND # 2 FAMILY SHOPPING

Mark, Ashley, and Mark Jr. walked around JC Penny's so he could find that perfect gift for his father. He'd pulled his name in the drawing. He had thought of just getting his dad a really nice bath robe.

Ashley had pulled Sharon's name. She had no idea what to get her. As they looked through the different departments, Ashley's cell phone continued to go off over and over in her bag.

"Aren't you gonna answer that?" Mark asked after the third time it had sounded off.

"No, it looks like it's someone from work. I'm off, and I'm not answering. They need to just figure it out."

Ashley knew all along who it was that was blowing up her phone line. It was Randall. She'd told him that they were going away for the weekend.

Randall was from Greenville as well. He'd moved to Conyers, Georgia shortly after Ashley and Mark moved there. Coincidentally, he was also going to be in Greenville the same weekend as them seeing family of his own.

Ashley wanted so badly to answer the call and tell Randall to chill the hell out, but she didn't want to upset him. She was contemplating sleeping with her husband but didn't want her lover to suspect any foul play. She had promised Randall since they were sleeping together, she wouldn't sleep with Mark. So far, she'd stuck to that. Deep down, she felt like shit for it, but the emotions had taken control of her. She was in the middle of a web and didn't have the slightest clue how to get out of it.

"Honey, I'm going to go over to the women's department and try to find Sharon a sweater or something," she told Mark to hold down his suspicion.

"Okay, I'll call your cell if I need you. Mark Jr. can come with me."

Ashley was glad he suggested that because she needed to call Randall back as soon as the coast was clear.

****

Lance and Erika walked into JC Penney's after going in countless other stores. Lance had to piss like a race horse. He'd begun to do the pee dance all around the clothes rounder's trying to peep out where the restroom was.

"Look, I'm going to go in here and try on this dress. You go find the bathroom and make sure you come back to get me when you're done," Erika said to her twin while he fidgeted in place with his legs crossed.

Lance nodded his head yes to Erika. He felt if he held in his words, it would hold in the liquid that was screaming to be released from his bladder.

Erika got a ticket and walked into the fitting room and went in one door from the end. Erika hated buying new clothes. Especially from the mall. She thought all mall clothes were overpriced. But since Lance had been sponsoring her new look, she decided she would try a little harder to look for more appealing clothing. Struggling to get her leg out of her pants, she nearly slipped to the floor before grabbing the fitting room seat that was connected to the wall.

After catching herself, she could hear a woman talking in the next stall over.

"Hello?" she heard the woman say.

"Hello, Randall," she said again.

Erika looked to the side slightly because she swore she knew the woman's voice. She stood very still waiting for the woman to say something else so she could be sure. She didn't know anyone named Randall, but if she kept ear hustling, she would find out who he was soon enough.

"Randall, hi. I see you keep calling me. Where are you? What are you doing? And why do you keep calling me repeatedly?" the woman continued to question.

She was quiet for just a moment. Erika assumed giving her phone friend a chance to respond.

"Listen, Randall. I understand you miss me and you haven't seen me in three days. Baby, I miss you, too, but you must understand it's the holiday weekend. I'm with my husband and our son. You can't have all my time."

Just then, Erika realized she was listening to Mark's wife. She knew that squeaky ass voice from anywhere. But who the fuck was Randall? And did this mixed mulatto just call this man baby? This chicken making a fool out of my brother?

Erika's brain was going a mile a minute. She didn't know if she should bust in and confront Ashley's sneaky ass, or just let it go on.

Mark gave Lance a hard time as it was. It served him right to have a little miserable shit happen to him every now and again.

Erika decided to keep her mouth shut. She sat on the small bench in her stall, pulled out a Snickers from her jacket pocket, and munched away as she listened to the rest of Ashley's adulterated phone call.

"Randall, baby, okay, listen. We're playing a family game tonight. I'll play for a while then I'll say I should run to the store. I'll meet you in the parking lot of the bowling alley on Pleasantburg Drive at nine thirty, okay?"

As Erika finished up the last of her candy bar, she balled the paper in her hands, licked her fingertips, and shook her head.

"This sneaky little El Debarge look alike," Erika thought to herself. "I can't wait to get back with Lance so I can tell him about this."

Erika had heard all she needed to hear. She cleared her throat loudly so that Ashley would know that someone was in the stall next to her.

"Hey, I have to go. We're at the mall. I'll meet you later. Nine thirty. I'll see you then, baby. I love you," she ended with a kiss over the phone.

"Lord, this shit has got to stop," Ashley said out loud to herself after she ended her phone call. She walked out of the dressing room and back into the department.

The first sweater she saw, she grabbed in an extra-large and threw it over her shoulder. Heading over to the shoe department, she ran into Mark and Mark Jr.

"Hey, baby. I found this sweater for your sister, and it's on sale, so I won't go over the spending limit," she said in an upbeat tone.

"Yeah, well, the best I can come up with is a pair of house slippers and a robe for Pop."

"I guess we can head to check out as long as Mark Jr. has found his gift," Ashley said as they both looked over at him.

"I got Cammy. I just picked up a Hello Kitty watch off the table over there. It's fifteen ninety-nine, but who's gonna tell, Mom and Dad?" he asked while they all laughed. Tired of being at the mall, they were ready to pay for their things and get the heck out of dodge.

Together, they walked to the counter to pay for their merchandise. Mark Jr. just wanted to get back to his video game on his cell phone.

Lance had made it back to the women's department to retrieve his socially deprived sister from the dressing room.

"Erika, you ready?

"Yes, yes, yes, I am. I'm ready. Don't you leave. I have some tea for your ears, baby."

"Well, honey, you need to hurry up. You know I lives for the good stuff," Lance replied, trying to get her to hurry and come out.

Erika rushed and pushed her way out of the dressing room. As she rushed out, she grabbed her brother's arm, who was standing right by her door. She looked from the right to the left trying to see if she still saw Ashley anywhere around.

"Why the hell are you looking around like Inspector Gadget? What the hell is it? Bih, is the F.B.I. after you?" he asked as he zipped through the aisles with his arm still being pulled.

"Lance, guess who ain't been watching to see if they grass been cut?" Erika asked her brother.

"What?" he replied, he had no idea what in the world she was talking about.

"Guess who thought the grass was greener on the other side?" she came back with.

"Erika, these jacked up ass riddles you trying to throw out ain't working. Spit the shit out, honey. Do tell!" he yelled.

"Okay, okay. What I'm saying is..." she said before a slight pause. "Mrs. Ashley is sneaking around cheating on Mark with some man name Randall, baby."

"Bih, if you don't shut your mouth, you betta!" Lance shot back quickly. "You lying. How on earth do you have this information in the middle of JC Penny's?" Lance asked.

As they walked towards the exit, Ashley, Mark, and Mark Jr. came cutting in front of them through some clothes racks in the men's department.

Both Erika and Lance stopped in their tracks. "And speaking of the little cheating chickadee," Lance smacked out loud.

Erika had to elbow him to keep his mouth shut.

"Shut up, Lance. She doesn't know I heard her conversation," Erika said as they followed far behind their family.

"She was on the phone with some man name Randall. I guess he wants to see her. She said she was going to skip out on the family game tonight to go meet up with him."

Lance relished in Erika's every word. Mark always seemed to give him a hard time about his sexuality and even about life. Now he knew for sure not even his older brother was exempt to error.

They followed Mark and his family to the eatery where all the family was supposed to meet up at twelve thirty. If everyone was done shopping, then they were leaving. If not, they'd shop just a little more.

"Mom and Dad, you guys have everything you need?" Lance asked.

Both of them shook their heads yes. There wasn't much they needed to buy at the mall.

"Ashley, did you get everything you came for?" he asked his sister-in-law.

Erika looked at the side of Lance's head like he had just committed a crime.

"Uh, yeah, Lance, I think I have everything I need," she responded, looking at him weirdly.

Mark looked as if he'd gotten agitated by Lance's question to his wife. "Did you get all the butt plugs you needed while we were here at the mall, Lance? Don't question my wife. Worry about yourself," Mark let out harshly.

"You better watch what you wish for, Stedman. You just might be barking up the wrong tree with your shade, brother. Lance will leave you alone, but, honey, LaLa will rip your LeBron James hairline havin' ass up. You hear me!" Lance clapped his hands and hit his knee in all seriousness.

"Shut up, Lance," Erika warned again.

As they nudged each other, he mumbled. "Shit, he fucking with me. I didn't tell his wife to start acting like Monica Lewinsky."

"Oh, God," Erika complained again.

"Okay, okay. Dang, Erika. Well, you shouldn't have told me then," he admitted.

Lance didn't want to let the cat all the way out the bag just yet. He wanted to have fun with this thang, but if Mark kept running his mouth, he was gonna get an early Christmas gift that was not going to be in wrapping paper.

CHAPTER 8

FAMILY AMERICAN IDOL

The family had gotten everything they needed from the mall. Another year, another successful family shopping trip for Christmas. That was all Mr. and Mrs. Bell wanted. They knew they were getting older, and they wanted their children to hold on to the annual family Christmas tradition. Family meant the world to the Bells, and they were determined to have every generation in their family know that.

Once they had all come out of the mall and piled into the van, they headed on back to Mr. and Mrs. Bell's home in Mauldin.

"Hey, y'all," Lance called out. You know whoever got my name better have some diamonds or some pearls in they bag for me."

"Really, Lance?" Erika asked.

"What? Heck, I got a good gift. I just want to make sure I get what's due to me," he said.

"It's Christmas time. Yes, it is," Lance sang a song he was making up.

"And Jesus said don't give out no shabby gifts.

It's the time for givin', not the time to be cheapin'. It's the time that old Saint Nick pull down his pension and share with all his givin'. Come on, y'all, sang along," Lance yelled out to the family in the van as they all laughed at his lyrics.

"Lance, that song is absolutely horrible," Sharon said.

"It ain't gone be horrible when I sign that record deal, sister."

"Record deal. What record deal?" Mark asked.

"Don't worry about what record deal, Malcolm X. Me and Ricky Rozay will make sure you won't be invited to my release party," Lance said before laughing.

That last statement just about killed everyone in the car. Lance couldn't hold a note if his life depended on it, and Rickey Rozay had absolutely no idea who his ass was.

Lance was a bullshitter to the heart but would liven up your party at any given moment with his personality.

The things that came out of his mouth, only he and Erika swore by. But if you got on his bad side, you'd see more bitch in his blood than R&B singer Teyana Taylor.

"Chestnuts roasting on an open fire," Mark began to sing loudly. Wagging his arms in the air for the family to join in.

"Jack Frost nipping at your door," he let out in a baritone voice.

"Hold on, excuse me. Hold up a minute, caroler," Lance blurted out.

"What, Lance?" Mark asked.

"I'm just curious, do you know this Jack Frost? How he know where you live? And who he lookin for, this hooch?" he said, pointing directly in Ashley's face.

Every breath Ashley held in her body was gulped up in one big breath when those words came out of Lance's mouth.

She knew he was no fool and hated her husband, but she also knew deep down she was lying and being a snake. Was her mind playing tricks on her? Was Lance referring to her cheating on her husband?

She had no way of knowing with the drag queen look Lance held on his face.

"Shut the hell up, Lance," Mark and Erika yelled out at the same time.

His redirect was starting to work on everybody's nerves.

Mr. and Mrs. Bell sat in the front seat, listening to their children go back and forth with their conversation.

Once they pulled up at the house, everybody filed out of the van like sardines.

"I am so glad we out that van, baby," Lance said out loud, releasing his legs from bondage in his seat. For the last ten minutes, he'd been being squeezed in the corner of the back seat, wrestling to get comfortable in his seat.

Mrs. Bell immediately went into the kitchen and began to prepare lunch for everyone. Sub sandwiches and chips was what she'd prepared to hold everyone over until dinner.

She and Sharon were set to prepare a big pre-holiday dinner for everyone before game night started.

Barbeque meatloaf, ribs, fried cabbage, macaroni and cheese, collard greens, potato salad, pasta salad, and Greek salad all for the main course. For dessert, Mrs. Bell's famous chocolate cake and pineapple upside down cake.

Even though Erika didn't talk much, everyone in the family knew she was famous in the kitchen with her light skinned sweet potato pies. Just for Saturday, she'd made six. She'd planned to get up at five in the morning to start her batch of pies for Christmas day.

That menu request was twelve with four to sell to neighbors.

That was okay with Erika. That was about the most action she got out of her life in a years' time, anyway. She'd hoped that the New Year would bring her new experiences. Even if it was just sex, or a male friend, or a sex toy. Hell, she didn't care, she just needed more out of her life.

That was just what she was setting out to get as the New Year rolled in. To get her a whole life.

Erika continued to marinate in thought in the kitchen as she cooked. Everyone else had found a corner or hole somewhere in the house to chill until the festivities started.

Ashley laid softly across the king size bed in her and Mark's room that the Bell's had prepared for them. Mark was standing in the bathroom, shaving his face and grooming himself.

Ashley watched as he maneuvered softly through the room, shirtless. She began to think back to when they met. She thought of how in love they were.

She reminisced on the sex and the sessions they would have. She was losing herself in lust as the man who vowed to love and cherish her for life was moving through life as if he hadn't noticed a difference.

Mark had not swayed in his appearance, nor had he swayed in his love.

If he knew she was cheating, he was keeping that little detail to himself, and he sure knew how to play it off cool. As much as Ashley wanted to confess to Mark and beg for his forgiveness, she knew she would never do that.

Randall had managed to croon her so well that she'd fallen in love with him. She loved his grace. His passion for women and his touch were electrifying.

What had Ashley the most was Randall's back stroke. He tapped into the depths of her soul when they made love. If only for that moment, he always gave her the experience of a lifetime.

She always wondered if Mark were to change things up and not be so uniform, would she be able to be one hundred percent in their relationship again? Would she allow herself to offer her husband that saving grace? Would she be completely sincere in her love for him again?

All of this, Ashley had no other choice but to think about every second of the day. A decision was going to have to be made, and soon. But in the meantime, Ashley jumped up off the bed and prepared to shower for her date with Randall in just a few hours.

CHAPTER 9

TO PIMP OR NOT TO PIMP

John Carl sat on the back-porch, texting back and forth with Amanda. They'd been talking almost every hour since they met. He'd planned to hold off on speaking with her for a while, but as luck would have it, she texted him first.

Her words were full of sexual innuendos and her verbs dripped of lust. Conversation took off from that point.

John Carl:

"So, what do you have up for the night?"

Amanda:

"nothing much, just sitting around the house"

John Carl:

"Are you cooking for the holiday?"

Amanda:

"not at all. I don't cook."

John Carl:

"Wow, and you're married!"

Amanda:

"What's your point? You still want to fuck me and we haven't even ordered pizza together yet."

John Carl:

"Yeah well I guess you have a point. But keep in mind. I don't catch feelings for one and you're a woman for two. I'm guessing you'll be in love before the New Year."

Amanda:

"Smug bastard!

Gotta go!

Ttyl."

Just like that, their conversation had ended. John Carl had developed a hard on for Amanda. Although he knew the game plan, there was something about her voice that sent a tingle through his bones. Never had this happened to him before. John Carl was trying his hardest to shake that shit off. "One step at a time, bad boy," he coached himself as he talked down to his own dick.

John Carl went to take a quick pee and walked out to the garage. That was where he had peace and quiet to himself. That was where he smoked his herb and get deep in thought.

John Carl pulled out a blunt he had rolled that morning and lit it up. Smelling the green and watching the cloud of smoke just relaxed his mind. As he looked up, his uncles Jack and Jackson were walking up the driveway.

"Hey there, nephew," Jackson called out to John Carl.

"What up, Unk? What y'all doing here so early? Momma n'em don't look like they done cooked nothing in that kitchen," he joked as they all laughed.

"Aww... You know how we do, nephew. We gotta socialize and get it in before the games start," Jackson said.

"Nephew, how are you?" his uncle Jack asked.

"What up, Uncle Jack?" he said, chuckling.

"Loosen up, Unk. Here, hit this L."

Jack reached down into the small refrigerator that sat in the corner and pulled out a Heineken. He popped the top with an opener on his keys.

"Nah, nephew. You got it. I'm cool wit dis here," he said, raising his beer in the air.

"Shiddd... I'll hit that shit," Jackson said after taking a hard swig from his flask, handing it over to his twin, Jack.

Seeds popped and smoke disbursed as Jackson took the hardest toke off the blunt that John Carl had rolled.

"So, nephew, why the long face?" Jackson asked through clenched teeth and labored breaths, trying to keep in the feeling from the weed.

"Ain't no long face, Unk. I'm just chillin', man. You know how it be."

"Yeah, I know how it be," he said, hitting the blunt one last time. "I also know you can't put a dick in the ass of a nigga that don't wanna be fucked, now tell me what the hell is going on with you."

John Carl looked to the side at his uncle like he'd just dropped a load of shit on the ground.

"What the hell, man? Dicks... Men... What the hell!" he continued to joke as they all laughed at his uncle's analogy.

"Cut the bullshit, nephew. You know what I mean. Why you out here by yourself?"

"Man, I just needed to relax," he said, grabbing himself a beer from the fridge.

"A'ight real talk, Unk. Y'all know what I do for a living. Well, I got this li'l shorty from high school I ran into, and I'm feeling her. I mean, her conversation got me, man."

"Hold on, nephew. Slow down. Count from ten backwards, nigga," he said, laughing, hunching his twin over to the side.

"Let's reel this shit back in. Think of what you have," he said in a for sure tone.

"No kids, no woman, no major responsibilities, and endless pussy. You gone fuck that up for a female with a big ass and a squeaky ass voice? Nigga, please."

The three could do nothing but laugh. Uncle Jackson told it like it was. He didn't spare your feelings. If you put your shit out there to be analyzed, that was just what he was going to do. He was gone analyze your shit.

Mr. Bell walked out into the garage, joining the guys.

"See, nephew, you see this man right here?" he asked, pointing at his brother, Richard "Dick" Bell.

"This man has a conscience. He been married ever since Mary was pregnant with Jesus, but a nigga gotta have hope."

They all laughed as Mr. Bell shook his head at his younger brother's crack on his monogamous life.

"That ain't the life you want," he joked. "If you gone be my protégé, nephew, you gotta leave all them feelings and shit at the door. That shit need to be foreign to you," he said, lighting up a Newport.

"Listen, man, sex should be the last thing on your mind. As long as there's women walking the earth, you can always get it up. Your focus needs to be on your future," he said, giving his twin some dap.

"You looking for 401k/403Bs and shit, man. Safety deposit boxes and wills and shit. You feel me, nephew?"

John Carl nodded his head. The respect was always there between them. He'd always listen to his uncles as well as his father.

"Don't be trying to get my son to be out here in these streets being a ole loose dick ass man. We Bell men. We have respect and dignity."

"Exactly, my brother," Jackson spoke back. "That's the reason why my nephew here needs to listen to the words that are coming out of my mouth," he said, mimicking Chris Tucker.

"You take those little thoughts of the has been high school titties. You respect the fact that you get paid to entertain all kinds of those bitches. Then you grab your dignity into the palm of your hand as you let them all suck your-—"

"Hol', hol', hold up now, Jackson," Mr. Bell yelled out. "I'm going back in the house with my wife. She's about the only sane person around here right now."

With that, Mr. Bell walked into the house. Jack and Jackson laughed at the truth as they taught it.

John Carl's cell began to vibrate in his pants pocket. When he looked at the screen, he saw that Amanda was calling him and not texting. An eyebrow raiser for sure.

"Hello?"

"Hey, you. Are you busy?" she asked.

"No, actually I'm not. What's up? I'm shocked you're calling me and not texting."

"Yeah, me too. I actually have a question for you."

"Oh, you do? Shoot. What is it?"

Amanda cleared her throat softly trying to find the exact words she needed.

"I'm only getting younger," John Carl joked as Amanda was mute on the other end of the line.

"I want to know if you can meet me right now," she blurted out.

"Like right right now?" he shot back quickly

"No, like right now, this instant. Yes, right now." She laughed.

"Okay, I guess I can. Where you want me to meet you at?"

"How about in the back of Walmart's parking lot on Woodruff Road?"

"Okay, give me like ten minutes," John Carl said.

Jack and Jackson both looked at John Carl and shook their heads. They weren't going to waste any more of their ancient Chinese secrets with him if he wasn't going to practice what they preached.

Zipping through the house quickly, he kissed his mother on the cheek and said his goodbyes.

"I'll be back after a while, guys," he announced as he walked out of the house.

He drove in silence to his destination, trying to remember all the mixed up mumbo jumbo his uncles had just dropped on him on top of trying to convince his hormones not to take over and get a woody while interacting with Amanda.

When John Carl arrived at Walmart, he drove slowly, tying to text Amanda to see if she was there. She directed him to the back row back by the row of semi-trucks. He parked his car right next to hers and jumped into her passenger seat.

Getting comfortable, he sat back in his seat and unbuttoned his jacket. He looked at Amanda's innocent face and voluptuous lips. He couldn't resist the feeling that he felt. He'd never seen a woman so beautiful.

"So, Detective Benson, you on your Law & Order stakeout shit today? What's up? You wanted to see me?"

"Yes, I wanted to see you," she said in an almost whisper.

Slowly, she unbuttoned her waist length sports coat. Underneath, she was bare. Light and smooth and bare as a baby's bottom.

Amanda had come out with the intentions of letting John Carl practice his trade on her.

She wanted to experience the electrifying jolt of life he provided for these other women.

"Listen, John Carl. I don't have a lot of money. My fiancé not husband does, but what's his is not always mine," she said, looking down into her lap. "What I'm trying to say is, I've been missing a lot in my life lately. I don't even know what all those things are that I'm missing," she said with a slight chuckle.

"But what I do know is that since we ran into each other, I've thought about you. I've thought about the tone of your voice. I've thought about the temperature of your breath. I've thought about the smell of your cologne. I can't get you out of my head," she admitted.

John Carl's eyes lit up at her every confession because he felt the same way. He just didn't want to show it.

"Listen, Amanda, I don't mind giving you what it is that you want. I may even offer you a wandering wife discount, but, and that's a big but, I don't do conflict. So, if you can't be fully discreet then—"

She didn't even bother letting John Carl finish his statement.

She grabbed his right hand from his lap and repositioned it in hers. As he fed into her advances, he stuck out three of his fingers and she grabbed his wrist, hunching his hand to the heaven's inside of her wet vagina. She released a load of juices all over him.

She allowed John Carl to mix his hand in her magic for the moment that they were together. Their moans. The groans had them both on cloud nine.

The car windows had begun to fog, and their breathing had picked up. John Carl manipulated his way so deep into Amanda that he had thoughts of an orgasm, pre-pussy stroking for himself, but that shit wasn't right.

He bent his body down. Latching his full lips around her left nipple.

After wetting the tip, John Carl sucked hard and finger fucked her pussy strong.

Her explosion was one for the books. She'd released enough cum to camouflage John Carl's hand as another nationality, and he held it all.

Quickly, she unbuttoned his pants.

Grabbing ahold of his member, he began covering it with her pleasure for her to taste. Amanda did just that.

In just a day, she'd managed to whore her way into another man's arms with his sperm sliding down her throat, and she loved it, and so did he.

CHAPTER 10

THIS IS WHO I AM

Lance sat at the computer at David's apartment while he packed a bag. They'd already decided for him to come stay at the Bell house, too. Mr. and Mrs. Bell had soon come to grips with Lance's sexuality. It was either that or never see their son again, so they chose the wiser.

David had just gotten a new modeling job. Lance had helped him pick out a new agent a couple of months back. Since David had an agent, his modeling career soared. Lance told David every day, all he needed was the right team. Now they were on their way to Hollywood.

David was a little younger than Lance, but that made not a difference. They still loved each other the same.

Lance was David's first homosexual relationship, and he hadn't even thought of another.

Lance took care of David. No aspect of their life needed to be looked at with a magnifying glass. They were in their element, and that was the way they had planned to keep it. They didn't bother people and prayed to God that people wouldn't bother them.

Everyone knew that Lance was the flamboyant one. David was the quiet and reserved one, but if he got upset, he did have a temper that had been marinating in hot sauce for months.

If he had to read any parts of you, you'd wish you were dead. So, for Pete's sake, they prayed before going out each day that a bamma in the streets would not make either of them have to read them from their birth certificate to the death certificate.

Lance could be a little petty, so he lived to tell a bitch about themselves.

The only big hiccup that the two had in their relationship was Lance's brother, Mark. He hated David. He hated their lifestyle, and he just hated them to hate them.

Lance had gotten over it already, but some parts of his brother being a complete asshole rubbed David the wrong way.

David had tried and tried with Mark. He'd taken him to lunch. He'd bought him nice watches for birthdays and holidays. He even did his taxes for free a couple of times. Despite Mark knowing that David was genuinely a good guy, he still hated him and his life choice.

Lance and David had made it back to his parents' house. The rest of the family was all sprawled out throughout the house. The two walked up the stairs to put their bags in the room that had been prepared for them.

As they walked down the hallway, they passed Ashley and Mark's room. Ashley was still in the shower, and Mark was sitting on the edge of the bed, tying his shoes. As he looked up, he caught a glimpse of them walking past.

"You've got to be kidding me," Mark said out loud. He totally disagreed with the fact that his parents were letting David stay the night at their home. Quickly, he jumped up and went after them.

"Are you freaking kidding me?" he asked hastily. As he showed his disapproval, his veins began to stick out in his neck as he yelled. "My parents have got to be losing their minds."

"Shut the hell up, Mark," Lance said, stopping at the room directly next to his and Ashley's.

"And you're in the next room from me? This shit should be against some sort of heterosexual brother law or something," he said, blowing and waving his arms in the air. He turned to go downstairs to talk to his parents.

"Go in the room, David, and put our things away," Lance told David as he followed right behind Mark.

He and his brother rushed down the stairs like two little kids. They ran into the kitchen, both talking at the same time, trying to tell their mother what the other had done.

She could barely understand anything that either of them had said.

"Hey, Ren and Stimpy," their father yelled from the TV room. "Shut up in there. Mother ain't listening, and I can't hear my show," he yelled to his sons.

Mark rushed into the TV room to try and grab his dad's attention while he was talking.

"Dad, why is David staying here? Don't you think you should have asked the other guests first?"

"Asked the other guests?" his father repeated. "Mark, if you don't get outta here with that," his dad countered. "Boy, let me tell you something. First of all, this is my house, so I don't need to ask another adult about shit I do in my domain. Second, Lance is your brother, and the sooner you realize that he's not who you want him to be, the better off you'll be. Third, I aint going against nothing your mother say unless you want me to move in with you and Ashley," he finished, crossing his legs and picking up a cold Budweiser from the coffee table.

"Dad, this is just not right," Mark argued back.

"Well, if you don't like the fact that David is here, Mark, why don't you just leave?" Lance blurted out in frustration.

"Lance, don't you talk to me right now," his brother huffed back trying to get him to shut his mouth.

"You are so ugly and disrespectful," Lance hissed with his nose in the air. "It's mighty funny how you always got something to say about what everybody else is doing. You need to loosen up," Lance told his brother, pulling at the top button of his shirt.

Mark was messy as hell when it came to their family, but if you caught him in the streets, he'd be stiff as a board.

He pushed his brother's hand away from his shirt.

"Oh, so what the hell is that supposed to mean, Lance?"

"It means just what the hell I said. If you stop trying to dictate everybody else's life, you may be able to open your eyes to what going on—"

"Hey! Oh, wait. Hey, y'all! Guys. Come on, no arguing," Erika said as she burst into the room.

She had sat in the kitchen with her mother long enough, listening to them go back and forth. She knew if Mark kept picking at Lance, eventually, he'd let him have it. She knew deep down Lance wanted to burst Mark's bubble with the information about Ashley.

She didn't care either way if Mark found out or not. Her main concern was for Lance not to make a fool of Mark and Ashley in front of everyone.

If Mark continued to press Lance about David being at the house, he'd soon find out just how Lance felt about him.

"Owee... You are so evil," Lance huffed at his brother.

"I am not evil. But the way you're living is evil."

"And the way you look is evil, you masturbating reject," he spit back.

"Lance and Mark, really!" Erika tried talking over them.

"No, Erika. I'm not going to stand here and let him talk to me and David like we're not even here. If he that homophobic, he need to take his ass home."

Erika turned and looked at Mark with the "Is you takin' yo ass home or naw?" face.

Mark looked over at their father. He was face deep into an episode of Wheel of Fortune. "Hurrup, Anna. What the hell takin' you so long to get to the damn letter? This heffa gotta be able to walk faster than that," Mr. Bell was yelling out at the television.

He then looked over at Erika who stood near the kitchen with her arms folded and her head to the side. Lance stood right next to her, looking as greasy as a pork chop on Sunday ready to throw some more insults.

Mark shook his head, throwing in the towel on his argument. He threw his hands in the air, turned around, and walked back upstairs.

Mark had lost that battle, but he was determined to talk to Lance until he was blue in the face about the choices that he was making in his life.

When Mark got into his and his wife's room, she was sitting on the bed rubbing lotion on her arms.

"Are you okay, baby?"

"I'm fine, Ashley," he grumbled.

"Don't get upset with me. I'm just checking on you, and as your spouse, it's my obligation to have your back. So, in this situation, I say mind your own business," she said, squeezing more lotion in her hand to lather her legs. "I understand your argument, Mark. I know you don't agree with your brother being gay, but he is a person first, and he's your baby brother," she said, trying to explain. "Have you ever thought that he looks at you funny because you're heterosexual?"

"Ashley, that has nothing to do with it."

"Yes, it does, Mark. If you butting in his business, it has everything to do with it. His sexuality is not going to feed you, pay your bills, or rub you at night. I don't see what the big deal is. It's his life," she continued to complain.

"Well, I don't like it. The shit is fucking absurd."

"No, what's absurd is you sticking your nose in other folks' business and you have absolutely no clue about what's going on in your own house. You should try tackling your own issues at home before you go embarking on fucking up somebody else's happiness," Ashley continued boldly as she walked out of the room.

The thoughts she had in her head about giving her husband a little bit of her love had been quickly dismissed during their disagreement.

Ashley loved her husband. The earlier feelings she was having were totally real, but Mark's stiff ass attitude and messy demeanor were an immediate turn off.

Quickly, Ashley checked her cell to see if she had any missed messages from Randall and to check the time.

Erika came walking up the stairs, heading straight for the linen closet. More dish rags needed to be taken to the kitchen.

"Oh my God, I am so ready to get the hell out of this house, Randall," Ashely spoke on the other end of the bedroom door.

Erika jerked her head back so fast as she walked past the room, you would have thought she was a crash dummy.

"Two more hours. Lord this time need to hurry up. I'm sick of everybody in this house, baby. They argue like cats and dogs. And my husband," she said blowing out a mouthful of air. "He has gotten on the last nerve I had left for the day."

Ashley heard the floor in the hallway creek and it spooked her. She didn't even say goodbye to Randall. She just hung up her call and walked towards the door. When she entered the hall, she saw the back of Erika's head going down the stairs.

"I hope she didn't hear me on the telephone," she thought.

Erika hit the last step and flagged her arms, trying to get Lance's attention. When he looked at her, her t-shirt was crooked to the side, and her eyes were big and wide. Lance shook his head, filled his forehead with wrinkles, and started laughing at her. He wasn't sure if she was trying to tell him something or if she was reacting to the whack weed that they had smoked a little while earlier.

She waved her hand, beckoning for him to come closer.

Eventually, Lance caught her drift and headed in her direction. Quickly, she grabbed his arm, holding him at the elbow.

"Come on. Right now. I have something to tell you," Erika whispered.

As they walked out of the kitchen, heading for the front door to go outside, Ashley was coming down the stairs.

"Hey, where are you two going?" she called out.

Erika turned and looked at her and turned right back around as if she didn't hear what she had just asked.

Lance didn't have a chance to respond before Erika pushed him out the screen door and down the front steps.

"What the hell?" Ashley thought to herself.

"Lord, I hope to hell Erika didn't hear me on the phone talking to Randall. From the sneaky look on her face, I'm just about certain she heard me. Fuck!" Ashley yelled out to herself.

"What's the matter, baby?" Mrs. Bell asked from the kitchen.

"Sorry. Oh, nothing, Mother. Just was thinking about something I forgot to turn off at home. No big deal," she quickly lied.

"I may as well prepare to tell Mark everything. If Erika knows about Randall, I know she will tell Lance. There is no way Lance will keep that quiet, as much as he hates Mark," she contemplated.

The more Ashley thought of scenarios, the more her head began to pound. Everything that was going on was just too much.

Hopefully, when it was time for family game night, the tension in the air would have diminished to almost nothing. But that would be wishful thinking.

CHAPTER 11

DRUMSTICKS AND DRAMA

Hours had gone by, and Mrs. Bell and Sharon were all done fixing the meal for the family.

Mrs. Bell beckoned for Mark Jr. to run around the house and let everyone know that they could eat. The child took off in a full out sprint around his grandparents' home.

"Time to eat, everybody!" he yelled out. "Grandma said it's time to eat, so get y'all black arses to the table now!" he yelled out for everyone to hear.

Mark came rushing out of his room after that last call for action.

"Mark Jr, did you just say what I thought you said?"

"Dad, I said arses not asses," he said, laughing between statements.

"Okay, son, don't get put on punishment while we're on vacation, you hear me?" his father threatened, chasing him down the hallway.

Mark Jr. ran for his life. Right into the arms of his grandmother. She wouldn't let Mark hurt one of her precious grandkids.

Mrs. Bell, Sharon, and Erika set the table for everyone. All the food they had cooked together was all laid out.

Everyone had begun to file in, but oddly enough, no one was conversing. It was as if everyone had had a very long day. No one wanted to talk. It was quiet as trays and bowls were being passed around.

Once everyone's plates were made, Mr. Bell, the deacon of the family, blessed the food.

"Father God, I ask that you bless the hands that prepared this meal today. I ask that you bless our lives with this meal. I ask that you strengthen our belief in you, oh Lord. I ask that you provide us with the nourishment we need to stay strong and be warriors for you, Father God. In Jesus' name."

Lance cleared his throat before his father could finish his A&B selection.

"And Father God, I ask that you bless the tongues of everybody at this table. Lord, if Mark says one disrespectful thing to me, Father God, I'm going to need your strength to hold back my hand from knocking a chicken bone straight down his throat!" he spit out with fire.

"Okay, okay, none of that," Mr. Bell said. "Everyone dig in."

Elbows were bent, and teeth were chomping. Ashley picked at her food while John Carl held his cell over his plate, texting Amanda.

"So, Mom, do you think you'll start your garden again in the spring?" Sharon asked.

"I don't know, baby. I really would like to, but the way my knees are set up, I may not have the strength to do that."

"Aww... Granny, I can come help," Mark Jr. offered up.

"Thank you, Granny's baby. That's so nice of you to offer up your time," she let out softly. "I really wish I could get Sharon and Erika out there with me. My girls need to know how to maintain a garden when I'm dead and gone."

"That's not gone happen, Momma," Erika let out softly, looking down into her plate.

"Momma, you know I am so busy with Lace Fronts and Lashes, I hardly have time to do anything I need to do," Sharon complained.

"You damn right about that," Gerald let out on the side.

"Shut the hell up, Gerald. I know you not talking, with your part time testosterone havin' ass. Don't you even get me started," she lashed out at her fiancé.

That was a battle Gerald was not going to win. Sharon was already fired up. All he had to do was say one wrong thing, and Sharon would rip him a new asshole. He chose his first thought and just let her have that one.

"By the way. Speaking on Lace Fronts and Lashes, Ashley why don't you stop by and let us get you together one of these days? Out of all the years I've been open, you've come maybe one time," Sharon said as if it was disheartening.

Ashley had a look on her face that screamed not to talk to her. Since Sharon had done so, she felt she was obligated to answer. She was still irritated from the disagreement she and Mark had about Lance. She was also worried that Erika may have heard her talking to her lover on the phone.

Every other look she gave, her eyes glanced over at Lance. Each time her eyes hit in his direction, Lance was already looking at her with his lips pursed in the air.

"That bitch is sweatin'," Lance thought to himself.

Lance looked over at Mark. He was stuffing ham in his pie-hole with a napkin tucked underneath his neck.

"This old molly maid ass nigga," Lance thought about his stuffy ass brother.

Ashley broke the quiet and answered Sharon's question.

"Well, Sharon, it's not that I don't like your shop. You have some pretty talented stylists in there. I just have one hairdresser that I'm used to going to is all."

Sharon looked at Ashley with a blank stare like she couldn't care less what her excuse was. "Bitch, get to my shop like I said," she wanted to blurt out then laugh.

"Oh, I get it. No big deal," Sharon decided to say instead.

"Sharon, why would you want my wife to come to your shop to get her hair done?" Mark asked.

"So she will look good enough to attract a real man, idiot. Why do you think?" she spit back full of fire at her brother.

Erika grabbed her glass of juice, holding it close to her mouth with both hands. Her eyes peeked over the rim of her glass, and she sipped slowly, watching as the pre-holiday drama began to unfold.

"I mean, don't get your panties all in a bunch, Sharon. I was just asking."

"Why?" Erika let out quickly. Everyone turned and looked at her, surprised that she would even chime in.

"What, Erika?" Lance let out while laughing. "My sister wanna know why you was askin', Mark?" Lance finished.

Lance and Erika nudged each other under the table, watching Mark as he kept a clear face while his blood boiled inside his veins. Mark couldn't help but be a temperamental jerk. It was in his DNA. But watching him try to keep it at bay in front of their parents was the funniest. Once he started yelling and belittling someone, he demanded the floor until he had the last word.

"Well, if you all must know, I just was wondering because every time I see pictures of people that have been there to get their hair done, they all come out looking like Floyd Mayweather's daddy, so!"

Lance spit half of his juice smack dab in the middle of his plate while Erika burst out into laughter so hard that she almost fell out of her seat. Even Mr. and Mrs. Bell had to laugh at that one. Just to picture a bunch of stuck up ass woman walking out of the salon with a hairline that looked like a Wal-Mart parking lot was hilarious.

Sharon was insulted. She was hurt that her brother would even use that analogy to describe the business that she had worked so hard for.

"Tell a lie and shame the devil," Sharon yelled at her brother. "I know you just told a whole lie. You know good and well anybody that leaves my salon looks good when they leave," she continued saying while stabbing her fork into a chunk of meatloaf. For at least five seconds, she delivered a dagger eye from hell at Mark.

He didn't think there was any offense in what he said. He told her how he felt. It wasn't his fault if she took it the wrong way.

"The shade in the room, honey! The shade in the room!" Lance said while sticking asparagus in his mouth.

"Mark, that was really mean," Ashley said as she shook her head.

"I mean, what do you all want from me?" Mark yelled out, and the fireworks were about to begin.

The Kanye West in Mark was beginning to surface. The veins in his forehead began to pop and sweat bubbles formed and popped on his head.

"I hope your black ass die a slow death," Sharon offered up to her brother harshly.

"Children! Children, that's enough," Mr. Bell said loudly.

Sharon looked at Mark and rolled her eyes like a kid, Lance and Erika glared at Ashley with that "whore" face, David sat eating his food as if he had nothing to do with anything that was going on, and Mr. and Mrs. Bell looked at their children as if they were the craziest bunch in the world. But they loved them all to death.

Keeping them together was a challenge, but it was a challenge that the Bell's would always be able to conquer.

CHAPTER 12

LET THE GAMES BEGIN

Mark got up from the table. He had begun to get upset that no one understood where he was coming from. Everyone was so hell bent on ragging on him for his comment.

He went up to his room and slipped into a comfortable jogging suit then came back downstairs to prepare for the family game of charades.

Erika and Lance had sat next to one another on the couch while Sharon and Mr. Bell sat together on the other couch.

Mark chose to be on Lance and Erika's team. They had pissed him off too, but not as much as Sharon. When he sat down on the couch next to his mother, she rubbed his shoulder and offered a pleasant smile to her oldest child. John Carl had decided to tear his face away from his phone and he joined Mark on the young kids' team.

Leaving Aunt Beattie to be with Sharon also. Uncle Jack and Jackson were so drunk by that point, they didn't even need to find a team. They sat to the side so they could be hecklers to anyone that got their answers wrong or right in the game.

First up was Ashley. She'd volunteered to go first just to get her turn out of the way. She drew a "chili dog." Go figure, a chilly dog with the situation that she was in in her life.

She stood and grabbed the black marker. As she drew her bread bun, Lance nudged the hell out of Erika's elbow.

Quickly, he turned to the side to whisper to his twin,

"Now who dang-a-lang she trying to draw? Mark's or papicito she screwing?"

"Shut up, Lance. Not now. Not in front of Mom and Dad."

"Eww… You so extra with your politically correct ass," Lance spewed right back. He wanted to see some drama, and he wanted to be the one to start it.

"Ashley, baby, what is that?" Mark asked with his brow raised.

Ashly went from drawing a hot dog bun to a boat. Hell, nobody knew what it was. After attempting to draw a dog, Lance blurted out, "Dog pound."

She pointed as he said dog.

Lance took that for his chance to run with it.

"Dog house, Dog park, Dog penis... Hell, Mark's penis!"

"Lance!" Everyone shouted in unison.

"What? Hell, I was trying to guess," he said, waving his hand in the air at them all. "Y'all ain't got no type of sense of humor," he continued, popping up from the sofa to get a drink from the kitchen.

Ashley's turn was up, and nobody ever guessed "chili dog."

"Sit down, Ashley. You need to brush up on your Picasso skills," Lance blurted out as he was almost to the kitchen.

Ashley looked in Lance's direction and rolled her eyes as hard as she could before plopping her butt back down on the couch.

"Okay, who's next?" Erika asked.

"Well, I guess I'll go since my wife just went," Mark offered up.

As Lance strolled back in from the kitchen, he almost choked on his sweet tea when he saw Mark's stuffy ass standing up at the board, ready to take the next turn.

"Oh, this shit is about to be epic. I wish I had some popcorn," he said, popping his lips and sitting softly on the sofa, crossing his legs.

Erika looked over at her twin and shook her head. She knew all too well the face he was making. She knew it didn't mean any good. All she could do was hold her breath and close her eyes when the shit storm hit because Lance didn't back down from anyone.

Mark's card for his turn was a businessman. Mark started with his drawing. First, he drew a desk and a chair. Then, he attempted to draw a man sitting in a chair, but it barely looked like it.

Lance blurted out "desk job." That answer was wrong.

Erika yelled out "man at work." That answer, too, was wrong. Mrs. Bell yelled out, "time is almost up, guys."

Mark went on to draw a man in a pantsuit over to the side of the paper. Ashley jumped up, answering her ringing phone.

Lance yelled out, "A man."

Mark pointed at him saying, "OK," quickly. Again, Lance ran with that answer.

"Man. Black man. White man. Man in a suit."

Just as Ashley walked around the corner and into the next room, Lance yelled, "The man Ashley talking to on the phone!" and burst into laughter. Erika knew it was coming, so she burst out laughing right along with him.

Mark stood at the front of the room, looking confused. He hadn't put two and two together yet.

Mrs. Bell yelled out, "Time up. The answer was businessman."

As everyone clapped and made the transition for the next person, Mark went into the other room to check on Ashley.

"Hey, baby, is everything okay? You walked out on the game."

Mark had walked up on her so fast, she was in the middle of whispering something to Randall. Abruptly, her finger hit the end button, and she hung up the phone just as Mark started to talk.

"Yes, I'm okay, Mark. You don't have to check up on me like I'm a child. I don't understand what all the following me around is for. I'll be back in there in a moment," she said, full of attitude.

Mark wasn't sure where the recent uproar of Ashley's came from. He just assumed leave her alone until she cooled off. Before he responded, Ashley had stormed past him, grabbing her purse and keys from the kitchen counter.

"I just... I just need some air. I'm gonna go get some air. I'll be back in a little while."

"Why won't you let me go with you, Ashley? It's getting dark out."

"Mark, I'm more than capable of taking care of myself," she said, storming towards the door.

This was her perfect out. She needed Mark to get the hell away from her. She needed to go see Randall. She had had enough of Mark and his family. She was thinking of telling Randall that their relationship was over when they met, but with the slightest irritation from Mark, that made her want to change her mind.

Ashley jumped in her car. Mark stood at the front door, looking out at her with Cammy standing at his side. Lance was in the background not far behind, leaning against the wall, eating a large pickle wrapped in a small sandwich bag.

"So, you just gone let her leave like that? You ain't questioning that shit?"

"Shut the hell up, Lance. Not right now."

"Well, if you talking about not right now, then when? Shit, she left right now, so deal with the shit right now!" Lance spat back.

Mark turned, storming past Lance, walking into the kitchen. He grabbed a glass of water and stood against the fridge. Mrs. Bell came into the kitchen to console her child.

"Markie, baby. How's everything going?"

"Everything's okay, Momma. I'm coming back to play the game. Ashley and I were just talking," he said, trying to make an excuse.

"Yeah, I see. It doesn't look like you won that talk. Looks like Ashley gone," she said, pointing down the hall at the closed front door.

"Yeah, she said she was going to get some fresh air."

Just as he said that, Lance was strolling his nosey self into the kitchen.

"Momma, air on the porch, too, ain't it?" he asked, being sarcastic.

"Lance Bell, cut it out now," Mrs. Bell told her youngest.

"Momma, you don't have to ride around in your car with the windows down to get fresh air. I'm just saying. No shade, but bruh, I can see the wool in this situation that's being pulled over your eyes."

"We don't even live here, Lance, so what in the hell are you trying to say?" Mark yelled, frustrated that his brother was still egging on the situation with him and his wife.

"All I'm saying, Herman, is stop being a fool. That girl just made up that excuse to get away from you and your dry ass ankles, but that ain't my business. If you can't see the forest for the trees, then, baby, you need to get your eyes checked."

Lance smacked his lips, said his piece, and walked right back out the room as if he'd never been there.

"Mark, don't listen to Lance. He's just trying to get on your nerves. Call her, baby. Don't let her get too far gone. Get this phone," she said, grabbing his cell from his front shirt pocket, handing it to him. "Call her, honey, and let her know you want to talk to her. See if she'll come back. This is not what our family weekend was supposed to be about."

"I know that's right, Momma!" Mr. Bell yelled from the living room. "I haven't even gotten a chance to pull out my Jack Daniel's yet," he said, laughing.

"Shut up, Dick," Mrs. Bell yelled. "If you pull out anything, it better be a suppository. Stop talking crazy. The boy already in the middle of a crisis," she growled at her husband.

With that, Mark went into the other room to call Ashley's cell.

One ring. Two rings. Three rings and a few more. No answer.

Mark hung up the call, scrolling through his call log, giving a minute to pass before calling her again. As he waited, he thought of how he loved Ashley and what he needed to do to make their relationship whole again.

CHAPTER 13

CAN'T JUST LET GO

Ashley pulled up to her and Randall's meeting spot. He was already sitting there in his Black Ford F150. She parked her car about six parking spots away and walked over. As she climbed into the front passenger seat, Randall's smile got wider and wider. He was ecstatic to see her.

Randall was a thirty-six-year old, Puerto Rican maintenance man that worked at Ashley's job.

Ashley was an underwriter for a large bank's mortgage department. She'd run into Randall over and over at work. Never in her wildest dreams did she think they'd take their affair as far as they had.

She may have seen him from time to time on the elevator. In her head, she'd be fantasizing about how buff his chest was underneath his light blue uniform shirt. Or she'd stare at his name over his heart and wonder what the rhythm of his heart was. She'd wonder if his sweat tasted as sweet as he looked.

She'd wonder how big his...

But her thoughts would always get cut off by the ringing of the elevator bell or someone talking.

As soon as Ashley got comfortable in her seat, Randall was all over her. Ashley had worn a long skirt as they had planned. He needed easy access. He hadn't been with Ashley in over a week and he was jonesing to have her.

Before she could get out a full breath, Randall's tongue was down her throat.

His hand quickly eased its way up her skirt.

The coolness of his hands made Ashley jump as they slid up her thighs.

She let out a sigh of acceptance as Randall slipped his fingers deep into her pussy.

Her insides moistened from Randall's penetration. Passionately they kissed and held on to one another.

Randall's scruffy beard rubbed across Ashley's face, just the way she liked it. He let go for just a moment, leaving her alone.

He opened his driver door and hopped out of the SUV. He closed the door and immediately opened the back door. Before getting in, Randall looked up to the front seat at Ashley. "You coming?" he asked, climbing in and closing the door.

Ashley returned with a smile as she climbed through the inside of the truck from the front seat to the back. Before sitting down, she unbuckled Randall's pants, exposing his huge package that she craved.

She lustfully wanted his stiffness inside of her.

She knew that it was wrong to crave someone other than her husband. The explanation she gave herself was that it was just to get more sexual gratification.

What she got after sleeping with Randall was just enough to keep her coming back for more.

Ashley pulled up her skirt, exposing her bare, shaven pussy. She'd decided not to wear underwear to her little rendezvous for convenience as well.

Randall was already as hard as Chinese arithmetic. All he needed was for his woman to put her gushy all over him.

Ashley sat down slowly, bending her knees into the bend of the back seat. Randall grabbed her hips while hunching his hips slowly in her direction. Ashley tried letting inch by inch go in softly, but Randall had other plans.

After the first two slow inches, he went all in, ramming his dick into her wet pussy as hard as he could.

She screamed out in pleasure, throwing her arms around his neck. Ashley buried her face deep into his neck as she rode his sweet little tortilla ass to heaven.

Randall released growls that only a man full of sensual pleasure would. Ashley let out a light squeal with each pop down onto his dick.

With each hit came a splash of her juices splattered between their legs.

She rode and slid up and down onto Randall until she released at least three orgasms in less than an hour.

Their feelings were so intense for each other that Ashley thought she loved Randall. She didn't want to act on it any further than she had already, though. Just her luck that would be the worst decision of her life.

Randall on the other hand, would marry Ashley at any moment if he was given the chance. He knew the situation they were in, and if Ashley continued to see him, he was okay with being her side piece. He didn't give a damn about Mark. He knew Mark from school.

Ashley was glad for the simple fact she could still get his dick. On the other hand, she did want to work things out with Mark.

Ashley's mind had begun to roam. Randall could tell he was beginning to lose her undivided attention.

Slowing his motions, he removed himself from Ashley's pussy grip.

He laid her body back slowly between the driver and passenger seat. The top of her head was just about to touch the button and change the radio station while her legs were up, knees bent, meeting with the headrest.

Immediately, Randall buried his face deep into her vagina. Her smell and her taste was his addiction.

Randall licked slow and long. Ashley dripped fast and wet from his tongue down to his chin.

She popped her thick legs back and let Randall devour her like an animal. He rocked Ashley's pussy and smacked on her goodness.

He pulled and sucked on her opening. Using his fingertips to spreading her lips apart, he could see her clitoral horizon peeking out. That's just was what he wanted.

He continued sucking her pussy hard, then soft.

He wanted to drive her sexually mad for him. He wanted her juicy love to let lose all over his face.

He wanted her to love him enough to leave her husband...

Ashley released everything she had in her body all over Randall. It was as if he were swimming underwater, and he loved it. She slid and rubbed her pussy into his shaft aggressively, drenching him once again with her love as he groaned for more and more.

Randall had placed an overnight bag in his truck just in case Ashley were able to get a hotel. He grabbed the bag and gave it to her once they both gained their composure.

She went through it to see what she would use to freshen herself up.

The feeling of her pussy pulsating from the stroking it had just received was at the forefront of Ashley's mind. Not once had she thought about her husband, or even her son, as she carried on the way she did.

CHAPTER 14

SOMEONE'S ALWAYS WATCHING

Back at the house, Mark Jr. stood in the balance, watching his parents as they argued. No one paid any attention to him being right there listening to the allegations as they talked about his mother. Mark Jr. loved his mom and his dad. He had his own unique relationship with them both.

He also saw the body language between them lately. His mother was beginning to dress a little sexier and more revealing when she went to work while his father worked all the hours he could at work, and as soon as he would get home, he'd eat, shower, and go to bed.

He wasn't a fool by a long shot.

He wished his parents would just get their shit together. Neither of them had time to talk to him.

One conversation a week was all he asked. He was beginning to get those feelings in his penis that he needed to have those talks about. If he couldn't talk to his parents, then who could he talk to?

Francis Malena was a girl in Mark Jr.'s art class at school. The two thought that they were completely in love. They had had opportunities to have sex, but Mark Jr. backed out.

He really needed to talk to his father about the shit that he was feeling, but when would ever be the right time?

When would either of his parents ever get their own heads out of each other's ass enough to realize that he was going through puberty?

That time may have come earlier than they thought, but it was happening, and fast.

Francis instigated their sexual encounters every time they talked. She'd text him revealing pictures of herself daily. She wanted Mark Jr. to take her young loins, and she promised not to tell anyone.

Francis was Iranian, and her family did not play when it came to self-respect. So, there was no way she could let her family find out how she'd been asking a little African American boy from her school to pound her into adulthood.

Mark Jr. had found a hiding spot in the basement of his grandparents' home that he had made his own. It was Lance's old room but was empty now that he and Erika moved out and were sharing a place.

After all the commotion, Mark Jr. went down to his spot and laid across the bed. He hooked his cell phone to the charger base in the wall.

Scrolling through his contacts, he stopped at Francis's name.

He shot her a quick text to see how her day was going.

Mark Jr: *"Hey Fran. What you got up for today?"*

Francis: *"Hey Markie. Not much. Been in my room all day watching porn, kmsl"*

Mark Jr: *You've got to find something else to do! Lol smh..."*

Francis: *I found something else to do. I want you to be my first but you keep backing out! Lbvs.."*

Pause...

Francis: *"Did you disappear?"*

Mark Jr: *"No I didn't. I'm here. Just thinking. I want to do it as bad as you do. I just don't know if we're ready for that Fran. You're only thirteen and I'm twelve. That's a little young don't you think?"*

Francis: *Mark listen. If you don't do it, I'm just going to do it anyway. Look at this and tell me if this changes your mind. If it does, then send me a pic back."*

Moments later, Mark Jr. got a picture message. When it opened, it was a picture of Francis with no bra.

That was a plus heading in the right direction of him changing his mind.

Mark Jr. stared at the picture until he started to get aroused. He unbuttoned his jeans, pulled them down half-way exposing his small pecker, and he got up on his knees on the bed and started to rub.

The picture made him want to yank his dick off, but he couldn't do that. He just did what he'd watched on XXX movies. It seemed to be working for him so far.

Lance opened the basement door to go down to grab a bag of ice out of the deep freezer. As he grabbed the ice, he heard faint moaning and counting.

Lance looked around the basement and noticed the light in his old room was on and the door was cracked. He tiptoed his nosey ass right over to the door. He wanted to see what the whispering was all about.

When he looked in the room, he wanted to seal his eyes shut.

Smack dab in the middle of his old bed was his young nephew pulling at his little penis like there was no tomorrow, and he was counting, "One one hundred, two one hundred, three one hundred," and on and on and faster and faster.

Lance didn't know whether to scream or grab some holy oil from his mother to throw on the damn boy.

He turned fast and headed back upstairs as quickly as he could, trying fast to get out of dodge without being noticed. He kicked a flower pot that was on the floor, and that stopped him in his tracks.

Mark Jr. heard the noise and immediately stopped stroking himself. He looked over at the cracked door while pulling up his pants.

Lance made a run for the stairs and made it to the door just as Mark Jr. came out of the room to look around the basement.

Since he didn't see anything, he shut the door back and got back to Francis.

He laid across the bed and used one hand to take a picture of his small penis with twenty hairs to send it to Francis.

"Mark Jr.!" Mark called from atop of the stairs.

"Yes?" he yelled back, pushing buttons on his phone while sending the picture to his boo with the caption "Francis Melena this is what you are going to get from me sooner than later. Then you will be Mrs. Mark Bell for life."

Just as he hit send, his father was opening the door.

"Come on upstairs. Your grandparents need some things out of the shed," he said.

"Okay, Pops. I'm on my way."

He threw his phone to the side, not looking at it twice. He figured he'd get Francis's response once he got back.

Mark Jr. followed his father upstairs and got to work.

For the next hour, they cleared things from the shed, threw away old knickknacks his granny had lying around, and talked about sports.

Lance ran around the house until he found his gossiping partner. She was sitting in her old room reading "Breaking Through the Silence" by Author S. Chameleon.

"Erika, Erika, Erika!" Lance repeated, rushing in the room, whispering, looking behind him like he was being followed.

"What, crazy? Why are you whispering?"

"Shhhh..." he said with his fingers to his lips.

She closed her book and sat up on the bed. "What am I shushing about? What is wrong with you now?"

"Honey, keep this to yourself," he started, smacking his lips.

"I just went down to the basement to get some ice, okay," followed by another wet lip smack.

"Okay, Lance, hurry and get to the point," Erika rushed.

"Well, baby, guess who I runs into down there?"

"Who?" Erika sent right back

"Mark."

"Okay, so you saw Mark in the basement. Now what?"

"No, baby boo. I saw Mark Jr. in the basement. In my old room. Looking at something on his phone, I'm assuming porn. Choking the cotton-picking estrogen out of his lil dick!" he screamed.

Erika fell over on the bed laughing so hard that she could barely breath.

"Lord, Lance, you did what? The estrogen? Have you lost your mind?" she asked, still laughing.

Lance was laughing just as hard as his sister was.

"Girl, I couldn't run my ass out that basement fast enough.

I didn't want the Eddie Murphy reject to see me accidentally peeking in on him jacking off."

Just then, the door opened to the room they were in. It was Mark Jr. looking for his uncle John Carl.

"Is Uncle John Carl in here?" he asked, looking at Lance and Erika as if they were weird. They were both holding in laughs.

"Nope," Erika let out through a soft laugh.

"Naw, Li'l Boy Wonder. He ain't in here. Get yo ass outta here and shut the door back," Lance yelled at his nephew.

Mark Jr. shut the door, and another bunch of laughter came from the room.

Lance and Erika were just tickled with the new tea they had just discovered. Just a little more pettiness to add to their roster. Lord knew this family didn't need any more drama.

CHAPTER 15

NIGGA YOU WINNIN'

After the moment, Ashley had just spent with Randall, she was exhausted. When she got back to Mark's parents' house, her brother-in-law, John Carl, was standing in the garage. When she walked in, the smell of the most potent weed filled her nose.

She held her hand out for him to pass the L he was smoking on. She needed just that little nudge to get her through this night with Mark.

John Carl didn't say a word. He just passed the smoke and they spaced off together in silence. After about ten minutes, Ashley broke their little cannabis bond.

"John Carl, another year of drama here at the Bell' house," she said, laughing.

"Yeah, I know, sis, but what else would you expect? We love to hate each other," he responded, hugging her before she turned to walk into the house.

Ashley moseyed in through the back-kitchen door. Mrs. Bell was sitting at the table, peeling potatoes for the potato salad for dinner tomorrow.

"Hey, Mom. How's it going? You need any help?" Ashley offered up.

"No, baby, I don't need no help. But what I do need is for you to go find your husband and work that argument thing out," she said, getting up to wash her hands at the sink.

As she dried her fingers, she looked at Ashley. "Ashley, baby, listen, I know you and Mark got married at an early age, but you can't continue to argue with the man, then storm out on him. How will you ever get anything resolved that way?" she asked.

Ashley looked off into the distance, listening to every word her mother-in-law threw out at her. She knew she was right. She knew she needed to stop the things that she was doing that did not consist of her family. She just didn't know how. She didn't even know if she wanted to know how.

"I know, Momma. I'm going to go and talk to Mark right now. Do you know where he is?"

"No, baby. I gave birth to him, I didn't put a GPS tracker on his ass. Go find him yourself," Mrs. Bell said, laughing at her own humor.

Ashley walked out of the kitchen, shaking her head. She definitely knew where this family got their sense of humor.

Ashley opened the door to her and Mark's room, and he was lying on his back with a book on his chest, and he was sleeping.

She grabbed a few things and rushed into the bathroom, turning on the shower. She jumped in to clean her body and jump in her PJs before bed.

As soon as she closed the bathroom door, Mark's eyes popped open. No way would he go all the way to sleep with it being nearly two in the morning and his wife was still out.

Ashley came out into the room, towel drying her hair then wrapping it up. She stood in the door of the bathroom looking at her husband with his eyes closed.

The weed had to have kicked in because even though she had just busted it open for Randall, she had the urge to bust it open for Mark at just that very moment.

She hadn't wanted to do that in a long time, but since the mood had hit her, she figured she'd give it a go. Hell, he was her husband after all. She was just deciding to be a whore on her own time.

As she walked over to the bed, Mark could hear her footsteps getting closer and closer. He was trying to keep his composure and not let her see him sweat. He didn't even want her to know that he was awake.

He tried holding his breath to steady his breathing. Ashley groped a large handful of his sack, rubbing it until she began to stiffen.

Mark slowly open his eyes, looking directly into hers.

"Ashley," he whispered.

"Shhhh... Baby, don't say a word. Let me take care of you."

With that, Ashley went down on Mark, thinking about the way she felt when she was with Randall, but channeling that intense emotion through to her husband.

Her touch was soft, Mark thought. Her fingertips felt of silk when they grazed across his skin. Her caress sent a shiver down Mark's spine that drove him mad.

Ashley's nipples began to tingle as she watched her husband get aroused by her manipulation. She hadn't seen a pleased look on his face like that in a while. It made her feel good to know that he still loved her. She could tell in his every move. The way he touched her back lightly, she knew she still had him.

Was she going to feed into it and stop the affair with Randall? Or was she going to continue to do her but pay more attention to the man that vowed to love her for life?

Ashley had no idea. These were things she thought about constantly.

For now, she pushed those thoughts to the back of her mind. She wanted to enjoy her husband and enjoy that night.

Just as fast as Ashley had put on her pajamas, she was taking them right off. Mark could barely stand himself. He wanted to move fast but didn't want to scare her off.

Ashley grabbed Mark's hand and looked him in the eyes.

"Baby, we have all night," she whispered.

That was Mark's confirmation that he had his wife back. If only for that night, he knew they were in the same headspace at that very moment.

For the next hour, Mark and Ashley made love. Inch by inch, each of their bodies were taken care of.

Ashley licked Mark literally from his head to the tip of his toes.

Mark could barely keep a clear thought in his head during and after the service he got from his wife. He wanted to shake that shit off and give it all back to her and then some.

That was exactly what he did.

He took very good care of Ashley.

The light in the room was low and the curtains were slightly cracked open. That made a brisk cloud of smoke over the silhouette of Ashley's body as he touched her.

It had been a minute. Mark had been working out, but Ashley had not noticed until now. She raised a brow when he revealed his six pack.

Mark looked at the raised brow that her face carried. He smirked inside at the thought of her not knowing that he was just fine even after her neglect.

"Yeah, baby... You like that Billy Blanks body, don't you?" he thought in his head as he admired her stares.

In the bed, Mark was alright, but he wasn't an award-winning dick throwing champion.

He figured he'd give it a little extra this time.

Some of the strokes and humps he was serving up to her, he surprised himself with. She seemed to be going with the flow and liking it, so he kept going.

Mark rolled his body on hers until he was ready to explode. Their bodies slapped together hard as he stroked Ashley from behind just the way he liked it. Within minutes, he was releasing a load of creamy love inside of his wife.

Mark fell over on the bed next to her onto his back. He rubbed his arm over his face, wiping sweat.

He held his right hand in the air and yelled out, "Nigga, you winnin"!" and they both laughed and cuddled until they fell asleep in each other's arms.

CHAPTER 16

CAN YOU TAKE THE CURVE?

Sharon and Gerald didn't do much participating during the family game. Now that the game was over and everyone had settled into their rooms for the night, they had to deal with their issues from earlier in the evening at the mall.

Gerald was trying to keep a low profile. He wanted to be where she was, but he didn't want to be in her way.

With any little mistake on her nerves, she would blast him and let him have it. Gerald knew there had been many times when he'd played around on Sharon in the streets.

He loved her to death, but at times her attitude could be so overbearing. Sleeping with the other women gave him a chance to block out his family drama. After the fact, he felt like the worst scum on earth, but what had been done had been done.

Sharon immediately went into the bathroom once they got into their room. She jumped in the shower so she could relax from all the events today. She'd picked out her gift at the mall, and she'd helped her mother prepare the huge dinner for the family tomorrow.

Her mind, body, and soul were just tired. On top of everything she had going on with the shop, her fiancé was making a complete ass of her, and she was tired of it.

She wanted to love Gerald, and she wanted to support him. But if he didn't stop with the cheating and start supporting her, she was contemplating a breakup.

Afterwards she showered, washed her face and freshened up her lashes before putting on her pajamas for bed.

When she opened the bathroom door, Gerald was standing there butt naked.

"What in the Sam hell are you doing Gerald?" she asked.

"Sharon, I'm sorry, baby. Please forgive me," he said, reaching out for her arm.

Quickly, she pulled back. "Gerald, do you think that by you standing in front of me naked that I'm going to melt and just say that everything is fine? No! Hell nah. You got another thing coming if you think that's what's about to happen," she said, walking by him, pushing him out of her way.

Gerald watched as she walked past him, going over to the baby monitor to listen in on their kids sleeping in the next room.

Gerald waited right until she put the monitor back on the table. He walked over to the door and locked it.

Sharon sat on the bed, rubbing lotion on her skin to prepare to lay down.

Gerald walked up to her, still brandishing his birthday suit. He hadn't tried to grab a towel, sheet, or a pair of pants.

He wanted to walk around with his dick hanging out!

He wanted Sharon to want him! He wanted her to crave his meat!

He really was just horny and wanted her to have sex with him.

Little did he know, Sharon wasn't paying him any attention.

Sharon could care less if he walked around naked or with a monkey suit on. She wasn't buying his ploy to get back on her good side with sex.

Time and time again, she'd taken him back that way, and every time, he made a fool of her once again. She had had enough of his shit.

Gerald grabbed the bottle of lotion from Sharon's hands and set it on the bedside table.

"Gerald, what are you doing? I'm really not in the mood to be bullshiting around with you."

"Who said I was bullshiting, Sharon?" he asked. "Listen, I know I've done some humiliating things to you in the past. Not actually to you, but the shit I do always falls back on you negatively."

"Negatively? Nigga, are you serious? You stuck your little puny dick inside a million other females and you won't stop."

"Well, it wasn't really a million. It was kinda like a dozen or so, but—"

Sharon mushed Gerald's face away from her.

"G, are you fuckin' serious? Do you think this shit is a joke? Do you think that I won't leave your cheating, dry ankle, Karl Malone, granddaddy lookin' ass? I ain't that hard up for companionship. You really got me fucked up. I am a beautiful black woman. I could have you replaced in hours. I refuse to continue to let you waste my time."

Before reacting to half of her comment, he had to laugh because she had just sneak dissed him, and she didn't think he heard it.

"Well, first of all, my ankles are dry. But that's only because you had to use it all on your beard. But for real," he said as he laughed and she smiled as they both were deterring this argument into jokes and insults.

Gerald grabbed Sharon around the waist as she stood up from the bed. Her bath towel was still wrapped around her almost dry body.

There was nothing Gerald could think of to say that would make her feel any better about their current situation.

If he would have left off the last joke about the dozen girls, maybe she wouldn't be so pissed. Making light of the situation wasn't the right thing for him to do, and now he knew that.

Sharon tried to pull away from Gerald. Any other time, he'd let her go and allow her time to cool down. But not this time.

Sharon was feisty, and if she got too pissed off she would slap the Puerto Rican piss out of Gerald.

She couldn't beat him in a fight, but she sure would start it if he pissed her off.

Gerald had grown tired of Sharon playing hard to get.

"Sharon, I know you're pissed," he said, trying to get her to look at him. "Baby, I'm sorry. I know that don't mean shit to you right now after what happened earlier. But, baby, that was a long time ago. Like for real," he said, grabbing her arms to turn her to face him.

"I know I've said this to you before, but, Sharon, you know I love you. I don't know, I think I got a problem or some shit, baby."

"A problem, Gerald?"

"Yeah, I mean. Shit. Hell. I don't know what the fuck wrong with me. Sharon I promise I'm working on it. I ain't been fucking with nobody. I promise I haven't."

"Man, I can't believe shit that comes out of your mouth, Gerald. As much as I want to believe you, I just can't. You're a liar, and that's just end of story."

Gerald had heard enough about all the shit he had done wrong. He knew he was never going to get her to listen to him. He needed her to shut the hell up and stop talking.

Gerald got closer and planted his lips right on top of hers as she spoke.

She tried pushing him back, but he overpowered her.

"Sharon, you're not getting away from me, so stop fighting it."

"Gerald, I don't have time for this. Get your hands off me. I can run my shop by myself. I can raise my kids by myself. I don't have time for your shit," she spoke back with fire and tears in her eyes.

She tried yanking away from him, but his fingers were planted deep into her arm.

"Sharon, I'm not letting you go until you listen to me."

"Tell the bitches you be laying up with to listen to you. I'm deaf to your bullshit now, Gerald."

Gerald turned to the side, rubbing his hands over his face, trying to think of any other strategy to get her to calm down and listen to him. To just take him seriously was all he wanted. It was about time Gerald took things into his own hands.

He was tired of worrying about what Sharon would say, or what Sharon would think, or how Sharon would react. He loved her to death, but she treated him as if he were an infant.

With other women, he didn't have that. He had a chance to show his masculinity, and that alone made him see other women more.

This time, Gerald was not taking no for an answer. He'd heard what she had to say, but he was about to put his foot down, get some pussy, and watch his fiancée go to sleep in his arms.

With that, he grabbed Sharon by both her arms and slammed her down on the bed playfully as she talked.

Her body immediately tensed up. Sharon had bent to the side in case she needed to block an unexpected blow from her fiancé.

Gerald's attack wasn't quite what she thought it would be.

As she raised up from the bed, he laid his body on top of hers, pleading for her to give him one more chance, declaring his love even through all of his fuck ups.

Sharon heard every word he said, but still didn't agree. She wouldn't look him in the eyes or look at him at all for that matter.

"Okay, you wanna keep playing hard to get? You wanna keep playing these games? I'll play with you then," he said, pulling his sweatshirt over his head, dropping it to the floor.

Sharon raised up from the bed once again onto her elbows.

"Gerald, for real. I don't have time for this shit."

"What shit?" he asked. "All I'm doing is trying to have a sensible talk with my fiancée."

"Well, your fiancée doesn't want to talk to you, so why don't you find somewhere to go or something to do?"

"I will. Right now," he said, planting all his weight on top of her so she couldn't move or push him off.

"Gerald, move. I'm tired. I want to lay down."

"Sharon, you are laying down," he said as he reached down for the band of her pajama pants.

"I'm not having sex with you, Gerald. Move."

Gerald ignored all her pleas. He knew Sharon wanted him just as badly as he wanted her. He loved her to death and had no idea why he did the things to her that he did. It just seemed to be in his nature, but there was no other woman that he would want to spend the rest of his life with but Sharon.

She continued to wiggle around, trying to get   away   from Gerald's grasp, but he wasn't having it. She was going to make love to him willingly if he had to lay on her all-night long.

"Baby, you know I love you," he said, speaking directly into her face.

She pursed her lips and turned her head in the other direction.

As he talked to her, he eased down her PJs slowly. Once they reached her knees, he coached them off with his feet.

"Sharon Latriece Bell, I love you, woman.

You like the beat to my heart, girl.

You like the cookies to my cream.

You like... You like the hot water to my cornbread. Like the milk to my magnesia. Like the frost to my bite," he spoke out loud and proud, jokingly.

"Stop it," Sharon yelled out, laughing as hard as she could .

She could not resist the laugh that was bursting to come out of her. After a few seconds, she had to let it out. Her laugh sounded more like high-pitched giggles, and Gerald loved it.

"I got you to smile," he said, staring into her eyes. "Sharon, I love you with all my heart, baby. I swear I don't do stuff to embarrass you or humiliate you. I don't know what it is, but I promise I'll work on it.

Please just don't leave me. I don't think I can take losing you and our kids," he cried with no tears.

"If I could believe you, Gerald, I would consider what you're saying. But because I don't trust you anymore, and I don't trust anything that comes out of your mouth, I guess your funny ass is just shit out of luck, huh?"

"Come on, baby," he said, licking on her neck.

She wiggled, trying to get away but not trying to get away.

"Gerald, seriously, I am so tired of this shit. You can have this damn ring back and we can call this wedding off."

He didn't even bother responding to her threat of calling off their nuptials. His hand still probed below both their waists. He'd massaged his dick then forcefully inserted himself into Sharon's juicy pussy.

"Ahh... Gerald," she screamed pushing at his shoulder blades.

Gerald bent down into her ear and ground his hips slow and deep. Deep enough for his whole penis to be swallowed by her fat kitten.

Sharon just couldn't fight the feeling any longer.

She'd given it a good fight, but the heat she felt in her body was crazy. The moment Gerald thrust his baby maker inside of her pushed her over the edge.

Sharon threw her arms around Gerald's neck and took the ride.

He stroked her deep and to the left. Her hips gyrated slowly, mimicking his rhythm, taking his every stroke.

"I'm sorry, baby," he whispered into her ear. "Don't fight it. You know you want me to take this pussy."

The only thing Sharon could manage to get out was a slow moan.

"Yeah...You know I love you, don't you?" he growled deep.

Sharon nodded her head yes slowly. With every nod, Gerald dug deeper into her fire walls. He made sure he touched every single inch of flesh inside of her that he could reach.

The room was quietly filled with their breathing.

The moments of intensity rose.

Gerald's breathing picked up, and so did Sharon's. Both of them had forgotten all about the arguing that they had just done with one another.

Sharon spread her legs wider for entry and Gerald took advantage of it all. He forcefully slapped her spot making her juices make music around them.

He loved on her pussy with not one complaint from her.

Thirty minutes later, Sharon was out like a light in the bed tucked away as Gerald had put her.

He went in the kids' room, changing the baby's diaper and making a bottle in case he needed it.

Once back in the room with Sharon, he crawled back into bed with his bae, cuddled her in his arms, kissed her forehead, and dozed off just as he had imagined.

CHAPTER 17

URGENT TEXT MESSAGE

John Carl fell on his bed and nearly crashed immediately. He had had a full day. He was exhausted, and they still had another full day of family stuff to do. He'd told his escort agency he'd need the weekend off.

Instead of him being off, he'd found his own prospective client on the side with Amanda. He hadn't been able to get her out of his mind. That wasn't like him to fall for a woman. Shit was what it was. Sex. An illusion. A momentary fix.

But there was something about Amanda that was completely different. He wanted her, and he wanted her badly.

As he laid back on the bed, he got a text message notification.

He nearly lit up when he saw Amanda's name. He wasn't going to text her before he went to bed. It was almost three in the morning. He didn't want to cause any friction in her home.

Seemed like she was up thinking about him as well.

Amanda: *"Hey John Carl. Are you still awake?"*

John Carl: *"Yes, I am. Hey Amanda. I was just thinking about you."*

Amanda: *"Oh, were you really? I hope it was all good thoughts."*

John Carl: *"Of course, Why wouldn't it be?"*

Amanda: *"Just saying, I didn't want you to be trying to throw me and my big breast under the bus."*

John Carl: *"You think you're funny. Ha, ha, ha..."*

Amanda: *"Come on stop crying...lol"*

John Carl: *"So why are you up so late?"*

Amanda: *"Don't know. I couldn't sleep. Up drinking tea and watching QVC stations lol."*

John Carl: *"Oh lord. Did you just say QVC?"*

Amanda: *"Yes, I said QVC. What's wrong with QVC?"*

John Carl: *"Nothing I guess. My mother has been hooked on QVC infomercials since we were small. Seriously we give her visa gift cards cause anything else she won't use. She can use those to order shit she doesn't need off QVC."*

Amanda: *OMG! That is so funny. Well it looks like your mother and I are going to be best buddy's then. I always order purses from QVC."*

John Carl: *Well I wouldn't go that far but..."*

Amanda: *No biggie. I know I'm rushing but I was just kidding."*

Pause...

John Carl: *"Amanda"*

Amanda: *"Yes"*

John Carl: *"Are you happy?"*

Amanda: *"No"*

John Carl never sent Amanda another message that night. She sat by the phone for at least twenty minutes waiting on some type of noise or light blink indicating she had a new message. Just that fast, John Carl had dozed off. But before he did, he had gotten the answer that he needed to know.

Amanda: *"Hello…"*
Amanda: *"John Carl where did you go?"*
Amanda: *"Guess you're sleeping. Sweet Dreams."*

Amanda put her phone down on the bedside table. As she did that, she thought to herself there was one minor hiccup with John Carl. She hadn't told him that she was engaged to be married.

She knew he had seen her ring and maybe assumed that she was already married, but she was not. Her wedding was in six months. Although she and her fiancé already shared everything as if they were married, they were not. With the way she felt about John Carl, she may have been looking at postponing the wedding.

She and her fiancé had been having a lot of problems lately. He'd been doing odd things. His phone calls became more frequent all times of the night. He started to work later hours during the week and extra on the weekend, which he really didn't have to do. He owned the maintenance company that he worked for in Greenville, South Carolina and in Conyers, Georgia.

He ran the company in Georgia, and Amanda ran the company in Greenville. Between the two of them, they commuted every two days to see each other.

They didn't have any kids, but they always said that they would work on kids once they got the wedding behind them.

Amanda's eyes had begun to get a little dreary. She went into the bathroom to wash her face and brush her teeth. Slowly, she slipped on a small lace gown and crawled into bed.

But she didn't lie down before giving her fiancé, Randall, a light peck on the cheek as he slept. She curled up on her pillow in his arms and dozed off.

CHAPTER 18

DUMB AND DUMBER

Uncle Jack and Uncle Jackson were still downstairs in the living room, asleep. They had fallen out drunk hours ago during all of the commotion. They didn't care who had done what or what was even going on. As long as there was some food for them to eat to soak up some of the liquor they brought with them was all they needed.

Jack had begun to wake up. He sat up in his seat and wiped sleep from the corners of his eyes. He looked over at the other sofa and saw that Jackson was still sleeping.

Jack slipped on his clean Rock Ports and walked over to Jackson to wake him to leave.

"Jackson. Get up, brother. We should go. It's the middle of the night," he said, nudging his brother for him to wake up.

"Wait a damn minute now!" Jackson yelled. "Stop touching me. What the hell you want?" he growled.

"Man, if you don't get your country ass up and let's go," Jack said, stumbling from the effects of the alcohol that hadn't worn off yet.

"Man, we can leave in a few hours."

"No, we can't. I'm leaving now. So either you're leaving with me or you're not," he said, walking towards the stairwell.

Jackson popped up from the couch because he didn't want to be left to have to talk to everybody all morning.

S. Chameleon

"Hey, Jack, did you tell Dick we were leaving?"

"Nah, man, it's like three in the morning."

"Man, you so full of shit," Jackson said, walking up the stairs to his brother's room.

"Dick," he called out, walking up and down the hall. "Dick," he called out again, but this time a little louder.

"Hey, Uncle Jackson, Daddy's room is down there, but he's sleeping. Did you need something?" Erika asked, walking out into the hall.

"Nah, baby girl. I was just letting him know me and your Uncle Jack were leaving to head home."

"Okay, I will let him know in the morning. You guys be safe."

"Alright, niecey. Love you. Take care. I'll see you tomorrow."

With that, he walked down the stairs, and he and his twin prepared to leave.

Jack turned on the defrost. With one swift swipe, Jackson changed the same dial, turning on the heater. The two were always going back and forth with each other that way.

They loved each other to death but hated for the other to be right.

"Jackson, what are you doing?" Jack asked his brother.

"I'm sitting on the passenger side, what does it look like?" Jackson responded, trying to be funny. "Jack, don't start that shit with me. It's way too early in the morning," he said.

"Jackson, you have got to learn to channel your anger, brother," Jack said, hunching his glasses up on his face.

"I was asking because the windows are all fogged and you turned off the defrost to turn on the heat. That made absolutely no sense."

Jackson grabbed his head on both sides, shaking it, he was beginning to get a headache.

"Jack, shut the hell up, okay? Listen, here. There, I turned your knob back and turned on the defrost. Are you happy now?" he asked, looking at his brother for an answer.

"Thank you, Jackson. That was very kind of you to take the high road and put the knob back," he thanked his brother.

"Jack, please just shut up. If you don't shup up, I am going to slap your ass into next week, seriously."

Just as Jackson finished his statement, a police car was pulling behind them flashing their blue lights.

"Well, pull my dick and call me a fuckin' yoyo," Jackson yelled out into the car.

"Nigga, yo country ass done got us pulled the hell over," he said, looking through the rear-view mirror.

"Jack, if I still got this warrant and I go to jail, I swear I will rip off all of your damn fingernails when I get out," he said to his brother, serious as a heart attack.

The officer knocked on the window with the butt of his flashlight.

"Excuse me, sir, can you roll down your window please?"

"Jackson, don't say nothing stupid and make these people assassinate our black ass," Jack mumbled.

"Man, fuck you, and fuck them. I'm just trying to go home alive."

Jack had rolled his window down as far as he felt he needed to.

"Hello, sir," he said, looking down into the car and flashing his light to see if he saw anything out of the ordinary.

Neither Jack nor Jackson responded with a hello.

"Okay. License and registration, please."

Jack had all his information accessible and visible for times like this.

"Officer, my information is in the pocket under my radio. Is it okay for me to reach for it?" he asked to hold down any confrontation.

"Sure, sir, go ahead," the officer responded as if they were playing Mother May I.

Jack grabbed the paperwork and handed it over to the officer.

"I'll be right back. How about you sit tight for a minute."

The officer walked back to his car, and Jackson pulled out his cell phone to text Dick.

Jackson: *Dick, me and your idiot ass brother got pulled over. Don't know the outcome man but make sure you call me asap.*

"Nigga, I cannot believe you asked that man if you could get your paperwork. This is your damn car. They can't tell you what to do."

"Man, I just don't want to die. I don't know if that man didn't get no pussy before he left home. He might have blue balls and take his frustrations out on me. Hell, I don't know. But whatever the hell works I guess," Jack replied.

He didn't feel like he needed to make any excuses as to why he reacted the way that he did. It was self-explanatory. They were men with pride, but they were also men with families.

"So stay cool, Jackson. I wouldn't steer you wrong, brother," Jack finished.

Just as the officer walked up, Jackson was turning on the recorder to his cell phone.

"Sir, can we have you step out of the car, please?"

"What for, officer?" Jack asked

"See, this that shit! This that shit they do before they kill your black ass!" Jackson yelled out while taping. "As a matter of fact," Jackson said while fidgeting around with his cell.

Meanwhile, the officers were forcefully pulling Jack from the driver's seat of the car. One officer had already reached his hand in and took the keys out of the ignition.

"Oh, nah, that shit ain't gone fly. What y'all doing to my brother?" Jackson yelled out

Another officer walked up behind Jackson and opened his door. He pointed his gun at Jackson and ordered him to get out of the car.

Jackson stepped on foot backwards out of the car as he yelled loudly, "My cell phone is in my hand, please don't shoot me. You're on Facebook live. Please do not kill me and my brother Jack and Jackson Bell." Then he turned around with both his hands raised.

One officer let out a slight chuckle. "'Ole buddy here seems to be well prepared for exploitation, isn't he?" the officer asked the other that was holding on to Jack.

Jack was giving Jackson the dagger eye to just shut up.

"Officers, can you tell America why we were taken out of the car?"

"Sir, turn around and face the vehicle."

"Sir, can you answer my question?" Jackson asked again.

"Jackson, just be quiet," Jack begged.

"You know, sir, this is standard procedure. We had a call of a vehicle like this in the area that had just done a B and E. Once we run your information and everything checks out right, then we'll let you go," the officer said, handcuffing Jackson and sitting his butt on the curb.

"Well, why you pull my brother out the car like that?

He ain't did nothing to nobody," Jackson yelled again. "And have you looked at us? Do we look like we gone rob some damn body? This shit don't make no sense," he continued to say.

"Sir, please just let us do our jobs. I promise we will have this whole thing rectified in just a moment."

Jack was handcuffed in the back of the police car at this point. The first officer was still waiting for all his information to come back.

In the blink of an eye, they got a call on the radio of a 2009 Suburban flying down Mauldin Road at a high rate of speed. Before they could respond, the SUV was flying right past them. Those were the criminals they were looking for.

"Guys, it's your lucky day. Uncuff him, let them go," an officer said in a hurry to go after the SUV.

Jack and Jackson had just gotten saved from Lord knew what, but thank God they had because neither of them could have taken a beating.

Jackson was already in the passenger seat by the time Jack got to the driver door.

"Nigga, would you hurry up before they ass double back and change they mind? Let's get the hell outta here," Jackson yelled.

Jack drove as fast as he could to the condominium that they shared. Jack's was on one side and Jackson's was on the other.

"I swear I'm gone start taking the bus, Jack. You act like you ain't got the sense God gave you."

"Jackson, hush. You wouldn't have done anything different."

"Yes, I would have. I would have let your scary ass leave Dick's house by yourself."

As they pulled up into the driveway, Jack blew off just about the whole conversation of Jackson's.

"Be ready at nine in the morning, Jackson. We have to go to church."

"If you say one more word, I'm gonna murder you, and I don't think God will forgive that. Now get the hell away from me."

With that, Jackson walked into his home, and so did Jack.

Their evening had finally ended almost on a perfect note, but with a slight hiccup. But tomorrow was a new day.

CHAPTER 19

TITHES AND OFFERING

Back at the Bell house, the whole family was running around getting ready for church. Mr. Bell was a deacon, and he hated being late for worship.

Mrs. Bell wanted to stay home and finish cooking, but Mr. Bell wouldn't hear of it. Tradition was for the whole family, and they were going to church.

Fifteen minutes later, everyone was ready to head out. Mr. Bell still had the fifteen-passenger van that he'd rented for them to go shopping in. Those that were left at the house squeezed into the van. John Carl refused to get in the van and wrinkle his new Armani pantsuit. He opted to drive his car with strict instructions from Mr. Bell to follow directly behind the van with no detours.

When they got to the church, Mr. Bell had ten minutes to get on his post. He opened the van door for Mrs. Bell and headed into the back door of the church to get ready. Mrs. Bell and the children came through the front door.

The family was seated in a row that would fit their whole family. As they were being seated, they saw Aunt Dottie. She hadn't been over all weekend. She always waited until the last day. She was always busy sleeping with this one and sleeping with that one. She didn't have time for lollygagging with the family, she didn't have time to gift-swap, and she didn't have time to help cook anything for the meal.

Aunt Dottie got up and moved her seat to the row the rest of the family had been seated on.

When Mrs. Bell saw her coming, she waited to give her a hug before being seated. Aunt Dottie hugged Mrs. Bell and kissed her on the cheek.

"Hey, sister-in-law. You're looking good today. Good to see you," Dottie told Mrs. Bell.

"Hey, baby, how you doing? It's so good to see that you could make it."

"Yeah, well, it wasn't by choice. I would have rather stayed in my bed, but I didn't want to hear my brother's mouth until next Christmas. Now, what time you say this gone be over?" she asked, looking over her glasses at the church choir that sat in the choir stand.

"Service should be over about one thirty."

"One thirty! That's too long. I knew I should have stayed at home."

"Shhh... Dottie," Mrs. Bell coached.

"What you shushing me for? Almost everybody up in here is sinners. I seen most of them at the club last night. We just happen to be at the same place at the same time. Now, don't get me started," Aunt Dottie said almost loud enough for the whole back of the church to hear.

As they were being seated, the deacons were coming out to get service started. Mr. Bell was the first deacon to walk down the middle aisle with an offering plate in his hands.

"Look at this ole bean pie eatin', raid outfit wearing—"

"Dottie, hush," Mrs. Bell bellowed out.

"What I do? I was just giving my brother a compliment as he walked down the aisle."

"Not in church, Dottie, at least wait until we get to our house before you go in on your brother."

Dottie did as she was told and shut her mouth. She sat quietly through most of the service.

There were about twenty minutes left in the service. The offering trays were coming back around for a third time. Dottie had already complained on the second go around.

This time, Aunt Beattie weighed in. When the offering plate got around to her, she just stared at it while Mrs. Bell held it out for her.

Her lips smacked and her eyes rolled as she looked at her sister-in-law with an inquisitive stare.

"What that for?" Aunt Beattie asked.

"You know what it's for, Beattie. Offering. Now put some money in the tray."

Auntie Beattie leaned her purse to the side and began to shake it. She needed any loose change she had to fall into her hand. She wasn't giving them any more green, but they could get some change.

"I just gave they ass five dollars already. Two dollars and fifty cents the first time and two dollars and fifty cents the second time. What they thank this is? I ain't got one dollar bills like a stripper," she said, still digging in her purse.

"I ain't got no more pesos to give these suckas. As a matter of fact, I need to know if I can make a loan," she said, digging her hand into the offering plate to take what she needed.

Mrs. Bell reached over and smacked her hand. "No, no. Put that back," she said, now snatching the basket from her sister-in-law's hand.

"Well, you can take the basket, then. I said I ain't got nothing else to give," Aunt Beattie said, stuffing the tray right back in Mrs. Bell's hand.

"I honestly feel like I'm at the casino. You know when you put a fifty-dollar bill in the machine, and within twelve seconds, it's gone and you still didn't win it big? Well, I ain't gone see no change from my first contribution or my second," she said, laughing, making the people in the row ahead turn around to gawk at her.

Aunt Beattie tapped Aunt Dottie on the arm.

"Dottie, now you know we should have sat church out today, don't you?"

"I know, Beattie. I am so ready to go" she said, scratching her leg underneath her skirt.

"I know one thing, they got ten minutes to either get this praise team crunk or I'm leaving. I can't take it no more. I feel like I'm at the Bingo hall."

"Oh my God, would you two be quiet?" Mrs. Bell asked.

Just as she delivered that threat to her sisters-in-law, her husband was standing before the church with the other deacons.

They stood with their right hands out as the pastor stepped down from the pulpit to stand in between them.

Pastor started on his sermon and was well on his way to reaching his point.

His voice began to drag gradually. His forehead started to sweat every time he bent back and came back up with a scream into the microphone.

The more he got worked up, the more you could hear the preacher squall starting to come out.

When he got excited, so did the musicians. The bass player stood over to the side with his guitar that was a tad bit too big for his torso.

The organ player. Well, let's just say he followed their lead. He was too busy in a daze staring at the choir director, Mrs. Thompson. He had a thing for her, and she just wished he'd disappear.

The young man on the drums was a little peculiar. Playing at a regular pace, he was sweaty and out of breath. Once the pastor sped up the tempo to open the doors of the church, the drummer suddenly went berserk. They didn't know if he was feeling the spirit or he was just rushing them to hurry up because he was hungry and ready to go.

He beat those drums so hard and so fast, you would have sworn he was trying to beat his penis to a porno.

The tempo was fast and the congregation started to feel happy. You had people running around the church professing their obedience.

The deacons, on the other hand, had a different agenda. They waited right until service got started and they were keeping watch on the office door to make sure no one was coming. As fast as the congregation was praying and prophesying, the building fund, the sick and shut in fund, and the just give us some money fund were being robbed blind.

Mr. Bell had stepped out to go to the restroom. There were three other deacons he left in the room to count the money and the checks. Unfortunately, they had more in mind than just counting.

Mr. Bell walked back into the office, and they had all their evidence put away so he wouldn't suspect a thing. The money was bundled, and so were the checks. They'd put it in the small blue bank bag for depositing.

Mr. Bell took the bag and shook each of their hands. "Thank you, men. I'll see you all next week Sunday."

All three of them nodded and walked right out the door in a single file line.

After Mr. Bell locked the money away in the safe, he went out to gather with his family once again.

"Daddy, service was wonderful," Sharon offered.

"It sure was, honey," Mrs. Bell added.

"Bullshit, y'all better stop lying to that man. That service was as boring as an Ashanti concert before and after she broke up with Nelly. Oh, baby, ooo, baby, oh, baby," Aunt Dottie sang out, laughing and holding on to her purse and keys.

"Who is Ashanti?" Mark Jr. asked with tape on the side of his glasses.

"Boy, go play in traffic, wit 'cho crazy ass. Somebody get this boy a helmet," Aunt Dottie yelled out. "If y'all don't enroll his ass in the school or get up to date in two thousand and sixteen, I know something," she continued.

The whole family had to laugh at that one. Mark Jr. stepped right into the lion's den with that question.

On that note, Mr. Bell escorted the family outside to the van. Aunt Dottie's mouth was beginning to get out of hand as usual. She could only last about an hour with no profanity. The kids thought it was funny that she had a curse word to go with almost every syllable that came out of her mouth. But Mr. Bell didn't make light of it on the church grounds, and he didn't like it. Aunt Dottie walked out with them to go to her car.

"I sure am glad we only do this once a year. The Lord would strike our family down listening to the way y'all talk in his house," Mr. Bell said to his unruly sisters.

"Well, if he knew what you looked like when you take your dentures out, he would have struck our ass a long time ago," Aunt Dottie spat back.

Mr. Bell gave a small chuckle and shook his head. He knew his sisters were a handful and they cursed like sailors, but he wouldn't trade them for the world.

Everybody piled into the van. John Carl and Aunt Dottie followed in their cars.

It was time to do their annual family gift exchange and eat the big feast that Mrs. Bell and her girls had prepared for them all to get full on.

It was the time for giving. The season was joyous.

Another year they had all managed to get together with a few minor setbacks and arguments. But at the end of the day, they were all still family and they loved each other.

The question now was if they could make it through the gift exchange and dinner without a hitch before everyone prepared to end their family weekend and head back home.

Mr. and Mrs. Bell had their fingers crossed.

CHAPTER 20

TELL A LIE AND SHAME THE DEVIL

Mrs. Bell had pulled out her fine china to eat on. She also pulled out the leaf for the middle of the dining table. The men got together and added it in for more eating space.

Everyone filed into the dining room to be seated for dinner.

Of course, Mr. and Mrs. Bell sat at both heads of the table and everyone else was in between.

Ashley sat next to Mark Sr. with a full smile on her face. After the night she and Mark had had the night before, she was content. She kept looking at her cell in her purse to see if Randall had called. Although she loved him and wanted to be with him, she had to try to work things out with her husband. She needed to tell Randall that and they needed to cut off their relationship for good. Last night was her confirmation.

After looking two or three times, she saw that Randall still had not called.

Mark Sr. had opted to make the plates for their family as Ashley excused herself to make a phone call.

She called Randall twice with no answer in return.

She figured he may have been with his family, so she would just leave him a message instead. She wanted to get it over with while she had the nerve.

Thank God he didn't answer because she didn't know if she would have the heart to withstand telling him in person or over the phone. His voice made her melt.

His voicemail greeting went on for almost forty seconds. After the beep, Ashley left a message.

"Randall, this is Ashley. I know we haven't spoken since last night. We were so caught up in making out that we didn't even have a chance to talk to each other. I've been feeling horrible lately about what we've been doing. I realized last night that I want to give my marriage one last try," she said, fighting off tears as she spoke. "I know this is not what you want to hear, and I hate to even be the one to break it to you, but our relationship is over, Randall. If I want to go to heaven or even see my son until he turns eighteen, I must stop this that we're doing. I'm so sorry. I hope everything works out for you. I love you," she finished before hanging up the phone.

"You love who? Honey, who are you talking to?" Mark asked, standing directly behind her.

"Oh, hey. Honey. Oh, that was nobody. I called my sister and left her a message. I hadn't spoken with her in about a week. I figured since it was the holiday, I'd call her."

Lance came walking into the kitchen just as Ashley was finishing up the lie she was serving up to her husband.

Lance popped his behind right past them, ear hustling so hard that he almost slipped on some water on the floor.

"Oh, my God, Lance, are you okay?" Ashley asked, running after him to catch his fall.

"I'm sure to get out of her and her husband's conversation." "Oh, I'm okay. I just felt the Holy Spirit touch me when you said you called to tell your sister you loved her," he said, grabbing the pit of his stomach as he talked.

"I thought you hated your sister. Didn't she steal your checks, wreck your car, break in your house to make a bologna sandwich, and take a nap? Don't she got like two and a half kids in foster care?" Lance continued to probe without taking a breath.

"Two and a half kids?" Mark repeated, scrunching his face up at the questioning.

"Uh, yes to all of those, Lance," Ashley spat. "Now what's your point, golden boy?" she argued back at Lance.

"Oh, hold the phone, Phylicia Rashad! I was just asking. Don't try to get fly 'cause I will spill all your little tea all over this place, honey."

"Baby, what is he talking about?" Mark asked.

"Honey, I have no idea. Like we said yesterday, just pay Lance no mind. You know how silly he is."

"Yeah, I might be silly but I ain't no fool. Fools wear suits and call themselves husbands," he said, walking past Mark, stopping to straighten out his brother's tie while dishing dirt on his sister-in-law.

Ashley tried to laugh off Lance's last comment. The whole thing went over Mark's head. He had just recently gotten her to give him some of her sweet cookie. He wasn't going to probe into the questioning further and mess that up. But Lance, on the other hand, had just confirmed to Ashley that he knew more than he should about her. All she could think in her head was that she was glad she had just ended things with Randall so her problems were all over. Or so she thought.

John Carl was in the sitting room talking to Amanda on the phone.

Amanda was at home in the basement relaxing, watching reruns of Law & Order: SVU.

Randall was upstairs in his office doing whatever it was that he did. The two spent time together every two days, but the love was gone. Most of their conversation was about Randall's business. The right hand couldn't do anything without the left hand in Randall's Maintenance business.

Randall and Amanda had been together so long that it was like second nature for them to work together. After the first three years, they noticed the romance had all but deteriorated. Most of the reason was because Randall had been sleeping with Ashley the whole time they were together.

He loved Amanda, and he loved her work ethic, but the sex was just not what he craved. Her conversation was not deep enough for him. The challenge had been gone from their union. But neither of them were in the position to break the other's heart.

Randall craved Ashley every day, all day. She had gotten into his head space. At any given moment, he would be willing to drop Amanda at the curb where he found her in order to be with Ashley. Only if she would leave her husband.

Randall sat in his office going through his cell phone. After he checked his messages, he was going to call Ashley to wish her a merry Christmas in hopes that they could see each other. After that, he needed to get dressed.

He'd volunteered to play Santa Claus at the family shelter in town. Every now and again, Randall had to commit to random acts of kindness to sponsors that backed his companies. It wouldn't have been a first choice for Randall, but he didn't mind one bit.

He scrolled through his texts and saw that he didn't have anything from Ashley. He did see that he had a missed call from her which prompted him to check his voicemail messages.

Randall pushed the button and began to listen to the message that Ashley left him.

"Randall, this is Ashley. I know we haven't spoken since last night. We were so caught up in making out that we didn't even have a chance to talk to each other. I've been feeling horrible lately about what we've been doing. I realized last night that I want to give my marriage one last try. I know this is not what you want to hear. I hate to even be the one to break it to you, but our relationship is over, Randall. If I want to go to heaven or even see my son until he turns eighteen, I must stop this that we're doing. I'm so sorry. I hope everything works out for you. I love you."

Randall bent down, retrieving a fifth of vodka from his desk drawer. Quickly, he poured up a shot and threw it all the way down his throat, swallowing simultaneously. He continued that routine about three more times.

His head was spinning.

His heart was racing.

His pressure had begun to rise from anxiety. Immediately, a migraine set in and his temples rapidly thumped behind his eye sockets.

Randall rubbed his sweaty palms together then covered his face as his elbows rested on his knees while he took a moment to think.

"No. This can't be right. This has got to be wrong. I know she doesn't mean that. God, if I could just talk to her one last time. I swear I will do right by her. God, please bring her back," he whimpered to himself as he continued drinking.

A few rooms away, there were no tears being shed. Amanda was still on the phone, cake mixing with John Carl. Her fiancé was in the other room crying like a bitch over another woman while she was having phone sex with an old classmate that she craved to fill her up.

"You know I want to see you, don't you?" John Carl asked.

"I want to see you, too, John Carl. It seems like we've been doing this forever. I can't get you out of my head," she whispered softly, slipping her hand into her pants, sliding her fingers down to her vagina as she licked her full lips.

"Amanda," he sang out softly.

"Yes…" she whimpered again.

"Are you being a bad girl?"

"I'm being a very bad girl, baby. I could use your help."

"Just one moment, baby."

John Carl set his cell phone down on the living room table and walked in the other room for a moment. Rushing back to his cell, he picked it back up, taking his seat back on the couch.

"Hey, pretty lady."

"That would be me!" she squalled into the phone receiver.

John Carl let out a slight chuckle at her eagerness to act like a child.

"How would you like to come over and have dinner with me and my family?"

"Really, John Carl? Are you serious? You would do that?"

"Of course. Besides, I'm the only elder sibling here without someone. Granted, they know I'm not gay, my father is starting to raise a brow or two," he said, laughing.

Amanda let out a light laugh at his humor. "Well, in that case, I would be honored. Can you give me about an hour? Text me the address, and I will be there right after I shower."

"You got it. Sending it now. See you soon, beautiful."

John Carl ended their call. His heart raced as if he were a teen about to have sex for the first time. This whole feeling thing was so new for him. He didn't know whether to feel good or bad about the situation.

What he did know was that in an hour, he would see the most gorgeous woman he'd seen in all his years.

This had been the most peculiar holiday season for John Carl. All he could do was enjoy until the thirty-first of the month and see what the 2017 New Year should bring him.

CHAPTER 21

PUFF PUFF PASS

John Carl, Uncle Jack, and Uncle Jackson excused themselves from inside the house. They retreated to the laundry room to get their minds right for this meal. With just the right amount of purp in their system, their munchie craving would be met all around the table.

The table had been set for about fifteen minutes, but for some reason, Mrs. Bell was holding everyone off for a few more moments. She said she was waiting for a delivery.

While the men waited, their chatter took over amid the smoke.

"You know, nephew, every time I see you, you got on these damn baby Waldo suits with no ankles and cuff links and shit. Nigga, don't you wanna relax?" Uncle Jackson asked, looking at him from the side.

Jack stood to the side, shaking his head. He knew the body gesture his brother was making. He was about to get animated. As he read John Carl to himself, he was going to need to do the facial expressions, the body language, the irritating voice mixed with a little of his own swag. Every year, it never failed. He always picked a new person every year to corner and give the tea on themselves.

"Unk, come on, man. Why you gotta start on me, man? Uncle Jack right here. Don't y'all hate each other?"

"Yeah, I hate that motherfucka, but you fresh meat. I can tell by the way you standing, nigga, you didn't follow my directions. Ya Uncle Jack ain't gone say nothing. He seen it. He smells it. You smell like swine boy!" Uncle Jackson yelled out as they all fell into deep laughter.

"Unk, listen. Let me explain," John Carl pleaded with his hands in the air.

"Man, I don't even want to hear it," Jackson said.

"Yeah, I'd rather not hear it either," Jack cosigned.

Jackson looked at Jack and rolled his eyes because he was no help in the situation.

"Nephew, listen," Jackson demanded.

"Me and your Uncle Jack done gave your li'l weak ass the blueprint on getting unlimited ass at no cost to you and no feelings to you. Your ass wanna get some old, school girl crush pussy and fall in love," he yelled, pushing his nephew's shoulder.

Jackson took a pause, grabbing a beer from the mini fridge, popping the cap. As his bottle fizzed, he started back in.

"Okay, so now what do you have? What have you offered her? Are your options still open to have a open relationship so you can continue to make your money?"

"Damn, Unk, you killing me with the questions. Is it time to eat yet?"

"Boy, if you don't—" Uncle Jackson started before being cut off.

"Okay, okay, okay. Listen. I just started thinking. It had been a long time since I had run into that lady that had that wow factor to me," he explained with a glimmer of sparkle in his virgin love eyes.

Uncle Jack smacked his lips loudly, disagreeing with John Carl's bogus statement. Jackson just went all in.

"Nigga, please. She reeled you in wit a camel toe and some oil. You a baby! You don't know nothing about this. Mark my words. Have a few more birthdays, nephew. You will see everything we trying to show will reign true right before your eyes," he continued, shaking his head at his nephew.

"Yup. It's going to slowly come down from the sky and slide all up in your personal space. It's going to be a bitch too," Jack said, putting in his two cents.

Jackson wanted to curse Jack out about his last statement, but verbally torturing his nephew was more amusing.

Cammy and Mark Jr. came racing through the house and out the back door to the garage, yelling at the same time, "Grandma said time to eat. Her delivery came!" Then they went running right back into the house.

Jack went walking towards the door to go in. John Carl followed with Uncle Jackson right on his heels.

"I bet you ain't even got the pussy yet, have you?" he whispered behind John Carl's head. "Nah, you ain't got it yet," he slid out. "She just let your li'l young ass touch it. She gone have a pacifier in your mouth in less than thirty days, I promise. Or better yet, she gone have you doing her laundry, li'l girl," he continued, picking fun as they walked into the formal dining area.

There was nothing John Carl could say to defend himself. Everything his uncle said may have been true, but at this point in his life, he actually wanted to take that chance to see, and he wanted to take that chance with Amanda.

John Carl looked down at his watch and saw he only had about sixteen more minutes before she would be there.

"Dad, I have a friend that's coming over for dinner. She didn't have any family to celebrate with, so I invited her over. She should be on her way," he announced. "Her name is Amanda, and I hope everyone can be super nice to her. I really like this girl."

John Carl not only made the adults laugh, but the kids even burst into laughter in the other room. Everybody knew John Carl was the family man-whore. The kids thought it was funny, especially because he got so pissed for people to call him that. When it started an argument with the family, that would be the best night of giggles for the teen and preteen.

Everyone sat down at their seats. While John Carl shot Amanda a text message.

John Carl: *Hey beautiful. Just checking to see how far along you are.*

Amanda: *Hey I was just about to call you. Per my GPS, I'm about eight minutes out.*

John Carl: *Okay see you soon. Everyone's waiting to eat*

Amanda grabbed her purse from the counter and wrote a note for Randall.

I'm going out with friends. Talk to you later.

Amanda drew a smiley face, and she walked right out the door, ready to enjoy her new little boy toy on the side.

Thirty minutes later, Randall woke up from his alcoholic coma, strolling quickly to the bathroom to brush his ratchet teeth. He strolled into the kitchen and made a cup of coffee on their Keurig. The note Amanda had written was sitting directly next to it.

Randall read the note, blew his coffee for a second, and drank it down almost in four gulps, quickly making another cup.

He had an hour to jump in the shower and be at the family shelter to play Santa Claus. He had no business drinking. Lord knew he hoped the smell didn't leak from his pores if he started to sweat.

Randall jumped in the shower, attempting to scrub off the vodka. He had to rush to get ready to be sure he was going to right venue.

Santa was all stocked and loaded in his Audi. He had the beard, the suit, and he even had a special package to deliver.

CHAPTER 22

TWENTY-ONE QUESTIONS

Amanda had found her destination and knocked lightly on the front door. Mrs. Bell went to answer, allowing Amanda to enter their home.

"Hello, beautiful. My name is Mrs. Bell."

"Hello, ma'am, my name is Amanda. I'm a friend of John Carl's. Thank you for inviting me to eat dinner with your family."

"Oh, baby, anytime. Anything that's ours is yours. Come on in here where everyone is," she replied.

Aunt Beattie and Aunt Dottie sat across the table from each other. They were waiting for the right moment to tear off into anybody's ass that got out of line at that table.

Sharon and Gerald had been sitting in the cut in their room, bonding. She had given in and let Gerald tear it up right, now they were in good graces.

The family of two had laid across the bed and started to watch a family friendly animated movie with the baby. About twenty minutes in, Cammy and Mark Jr. ran up with a dinner request for them as well.

Now that Amanda had made it, it was time for the family to say prayer and dig in to all the food that graced them.

John Carl and Amanda sat directly across from Uncle Jack and Uncle Jackson. He would have rather sat on the same side as them so he wouldn't have to catch their wandering eyes looking at Amanda seductively and looking at him as if he were a damn fool.

Mr. Bell went in saying the grace over their dinner. Everyone was required to hold hands through prayer. If Mrs. Bell saw one person being disobedient, it was out of her house you would go. Soon after, it was time to feast.

Large bowls and spoons were being passed, silver pans full of delicious goodness were being switched from hand to hand, and everyone was ready to eat.

The only thing you could hear ten minutes later were forks hitting people's plates and small talk.

"So, Ashley, how did you meet my son?" Mrs. Bell asked.

"Well, actually, ma'am, John Carl and I went to school together."

"Oh, is that right?"

Amanda shook her head yes, but judging by some of the looks she was getting, she needed to rethink her answer. She decided to just stay quiet and go with the flow.

"So, is you married, Amanda from school?" Uncle Jackson asked across the table.

"Well, Uncle Jackson, if she was married, I don't think she would be here with me, right?" John Carl quickly answered.

"Nigga, do you think I don't know what you do for a living? Don't try to play me like you ain't got titties dropping down on you from the sky on yo ass. Let the girl answer the question," he said.

"Amanda, don't answer that. Unk, I already answered for her. Can everybody just eat or change the subject, please?" John Carl pleaded.

"That's fine with me, while you trying to hold that girl hostage over there next to you," Uncle Jackson said, stuffing mashed potatoes in his mouth.

"So, Amanda, do you attend a church here in Greenville?" Mr. Bell asked.

"Uh, no, sir. Not right now."

"Well, we're always taking new members at Reedy Rock Missionary Baptist Church if you're ever interested. We'd love to have you sometime."

"Well, I'll have to keep that in mind," Amanda responded, looking at John Carl, smiling as he put food on a plate for her.

Uncle Jackson nudged uncle Jack and pointed at John Carl.

"Look at this ole pancake ass nigga making the girl plate. She gone treat him like a bitch for the rest of his life," he said as he and Jack laughed at the inside joke.

"Well, since you answering questions, Annie—"

"Her name is Amanda, Uncle Jack."

"Well, okay, Amanda, I want to know do you like men that suck they thumb?"

"And do you do your own laundry?" Uncle Jackson followed up.

"Come on, guys," John Carl said. He had grown a little tired of all the questioning.

Jack and Jackson were smirking to each other, watching as John Carl sweat for his life in front of this girl. He pulled out all the stops. He had on enough cologne to give your ass hay fever, and the pants to his Armani suit were so tight, it probably decreased his sperm count.

"Lawd, lawd, lawd somebody done put they foot off in these chit'lings," Aunt Beattie said, sopping up a slop of them onto her fork and stuffing them in her mouth. She was trying to defuse the situation at hand. She knew Jack and Jackson were either going to talk the girl right out of her clothes, or better yet, John Carl was going to kick their asses for making a complete fool of him in front of his company.

Looking around the table, everyone seemed to be in their own world. With all the attitudes flying around, no one knew what the evening was going to bring.

CHAPTER 23

LORD GUIDE THY TONGUE

Sharon and Gerald's baby, Poodah, was cooing at the opposite end of the table. He sat in his little high chair with his face full of mac and cheese, talking his baby talk as everyone else conversed.

John Carl and Amanda sat close and were talking. He looked deep into her eyes as she spoke to him, and she followed his lips as he spoke every word.

"Come with me for just a second, please," John Carl said to Amanda as he coached her chair from under the table.

"Excuse us, everyone. We will be right back."

John Carl and Amanda walked out into the garage, and John Carl locked the door so no one could bust in on them. As soon as he closed the door, he grabbed Amanda by the waist and threw her against his mother's spare refrigerator.

He unraveled the string on her joggers quickly, sliding his hand between her skin and the fabric. Amanda caught her breath at the feeling his aggression gave her.

She wanted John Carl just as badly as he wanted her.

As he had done the night before, John Carl worked on Amanda's pussy with the meanest handwork. It was like he knew every step of the manipulation.

He teased her vagina with the tips of his fingers until her body began to tremble.

Somehow, Amanda had let John Carl put the moves on her because she loved everything he was doing to her. Not one time did she ever think of her fiancé. She was enjoying the moment with her new beau.

Back in the dining room, Aunt Beattie was trying to have a conversation with her sister, but Sharon and Gerald's baby was cooing so loudly, she could barely pay attention.

"What the hell y'all down there feeding that baby?" she asked.

Sharon just looked at Aunt Beattie and continued to talk to Gerald as if she hadn't just asked a question.

"See, Dottie, that's that kind of shit I be talking about. These new jack ass parents. Look at Sharon, she a prime example. When you ask they ass a question about they kids, they get all defensive and sensitive and shit," she said, looking directly at Sharon. "Yeah, I'm talking about you," she spit at Sharon as she looked up at her. "You sitting down there ignoring me when I asked you about your baby. I was just gone give his ass compliment, but I see you ain't in the mood," she shot at her niece.

"Aunt Beattie, I don't have an attitude. I just know your sense of humor," she said, trying to keep their conversation cordial.

"You know my sense of humor," Aunt Beattie repeated. "Shut the hell up, girl. You don't know what the hell you talking about," she said, laughing with Aunt Dottie.

Lil Poodah started to coo loudly again. He had spit flying from his fingers, and cheese going into his nose. He was the most precious little black baby, Aunt Beattie thought, but his ass talked too loud.

"Sharon, have you gotten out your feelings yet?"

"I'm not in my feelings, Auntie," she shot back quickly.

"Well, good, you ain't in your feelings. Why don't you shut baby Huey up down there, then? His ass down there talking more than we is, and he ain't even been to kindergarten yet."

Lance and Erika fell out of control in laughter.

"I mean, I ain't trying to talk about the precious little serpent, but at the rate he talking, he gone either be a Kung Fu sen sai when he grow up, or a Spanish translator. What y'all think?" Aunt Beattie went on to taunt Sharon and Gerald's child.

Lance almost choked on his drink while Erika's eyes nearly popped out of her head. She just knew Sharon was going to jump across the table and suflex Aunt Beattie.

Those two loved when Aunt Beattie and Aunt Dottie came over because they knew they'd go around the table roasting everyone individually.

Sharon had had enough of her aunt's insults. "Would you just shut up! Daddy, get your sister," she shot back quickly with fire at her aunt's comments. Gerald grabbed Sharon's arm to calm her down, and she snatched away.

"Don't grab me. That old lady think she won't catch it. All she gotta do is give me a reason," Sharon threatened. "I been waiting to use my new Taser on somebody. She better step the fuck off," Sharon threatened again.

Lance scrunched his forehead in disbelief at the premeditated felony his sister had just admitted to out loud, but he grabbed his phone and started recording.

"Sharon, did you just say you were going to taze our old ass auntie? I'm putting this shit on World Star," Lance shouted out.

"I sure did," Sharon said with her lips pursed in the air. "I will fry her ass like a piece of bacon."

"Let me see you try it, Wonder Bra Wilma," Aunt Beattie threw back.

"You old witch," Sharon said lastly.

"Just one moment," Mr. Bell cut in. Trying to defuse any brewing blows from the family. "Can't we all just have a nice dinner? Beattie, you ought not do my kids like that. You bring your big greasy self over here and piss my kids off every single time. It's the holiday. Act like you got some sense," her brother told her.

For the first time since they'd been at the table, it was quiet. Everyone heard the seriousness in Mr. Bell's voice. He was not joking. His dominance would have worked if there wasn't other drama that was in the mix of being stirred up just as one mess was being put out.

Sharon got up and walked to the kitchen to get some juice. She needed to excuse herself from the table. She loved her aunts, but sometimes, they were just a little too much. She wanted to rip her aunt a new one for talking about her baby, but she would never disrespect her elders.

Just as she was walking into the kitchen, John Carl and Amanda were coming in from the garage. Amanda immediately went into the restroom, and John Carl stood around by the door waiting on her to come out.

Sharon shook her head, walking past her brother, headed back into the dining room.

There was a man in a Santa Claus suit standing on the sidewalk, and she thought that was very peculiar. She stood at the screen door for a couple seconds to see if he would come to the door.

The man just stood there looking up at the house.

Sharon decided to open the door to see if the man needed any help.

"Excuse me, sir, is there something I can help you with?"

Turning in a half circle contemplating walking back to his car, Randall turned, facing her. He swallowed his pride and went after his woman as he walked up onto the porch.

CHAPTER 24

SURPRISE GUEST

John Carl had walked into the foyer, waiting for Amanda to come from the restroom. There was a strange man in a Santa suit standing on the front porch, talking to his sister through the door.

"Hey, sis, who is that?"

"I don't know yet," she said, turning to look at the man again.

"Hello, ma'am, my name is Randall. I was wondering if Ashley Bell was available?"

"Ashley?"

"Yes, ma'am, Ashley Bell."

"Yeah, she available. Just a second, let me get her for you. You can come in," Sharon said, letting Randall come in and stand in the foyer.

Sharon knew damn well she didn't know the man, and the way he looked, she knew her brother didn't either. She rushed into the dining room and announced to Ashley that she had company quicker than lighting.

"Ashley, some fine ass burrito name Randall is at the door for you. He wanted to know if you were available."

Lance and Erika had heard the magic word "Randall." They looked into each other's faces with their eyes bucked. Lance began starting a new World Star video while Erika was sitting, eating sweet potato pie, waiting for things to unfold.

Ashley turned and looked at Mark. He was already staring at the side of her head.

"Really, someone for me?" Ashley already knew what it was. Randall was a fine tanned glass of Hispanic water that she loved to drink, but she knew that he had done the ultimate by coming to her in-laws' house.

She walked around the hall, and Randall was standing in front of the door, dressed like Santa, looking sad and drunk.

"Randall, what are you doing? You know damn well you're not supposed to be here. Why would you come over here?" she asked, grabbing his elbow, ushering him out on the porch so they could talk.

Mark was still sitting in his same seat at the dinner table.

"Mark, baby, you not gonna go see why a man is coming over here for your wife?" Mrs. Bell asked her son.

"Yeah, dummy, why you just sitting there?" Lance let out.

"Yeah, bro, don't you think you need to come check this shit out?" John Carl butted in from the hallway. "Shit, if you want, I'll go out there and see who he is and what's going on," John Carl offered up.

"No, that's okay, you guys. Just give her privacy," Mark said, looking embarrassed.

Lance scooted his chair all the way back from the table. "You the craziest married person I have ever encountered in my life, Mark. That's why she run circles around your ass 'cause you let her do what she want to do."

Lance was now standing in the hallway between the front door and the dining room.

Aunt Beattie and Aunt Dottie had a front row seat to the drama. They hadn't had their chance to chime in yet on the new visitor, but they were getting geared and ready to go in.

Meanwhile, on the porch, Ashley was delivering a world-renowned tongue lashing to Randall.

She was absolutely furious that he had come to her in-laws' house. She thought by leaving him the message she left, that she would be able to just put an end to their five-year relationship.

Randall was not accepting that, and Ashley was beginning to find that out.

"Don't you know that my husband and my child are here?" Ashley asked Randall.

"Ashley I know that, and I am so sorry for disrespecting your family and coming over here unannounced."

"Well, good then. Get in your car and get the hell out of here. I'm not going to do this with you, Randall. I said what I had to say. There is nothing else we need to talk about."

"Ashley, what do you mean?" he asked, waving his arms in the air, frustrated.

"So, you're telling me that you can just walk away from us like that?"

"Randall, what the fuck do you mean? You knew what it was from the beginning. I can't believe after all the times that we've talked about this, you're still acting like an oversexed juvenile. This is not what I wanted, and you know that," she yelled into Randall's face.

He was taken aback by her sudden onset of anger. He had never seen Ashley be so aggressive. It kind of turned him on, but now was not the time for that.

"Ashley, please. Can you and I just go somewhere and sit down so we can talk?"

"Randall, no. I'm sorry you have to go," she said, pulling on the screen door to go back into the house. Randall was hot on her trail. Ashley released the screen door, and he grabbed it and walked into the house right behind her.

"Randall, fucking stop it already. Now I've had enough. Go home!" she yelled into his face.

Just then, Amanda was coming back from the restroom. She was looking down at her hands as she dried them with a paper towel.

When she looked up, her eyes fell on the man that she shared her bed with almost every other night.

"Randall," Amanda said, looking at him, shocked to see him there. She didn't know if he had come to bust her out or if he was just being a weirdo going over to people's houses dressed like Santa Claus.

"Amanda! What are you doing here? You know these people?"

"These people. Hold up, bruh," John Carl said, stepping up to defend the title of his family. "Who the hell are you, and why you in my parents' house even asking questions?" John Carl continued. "So, Amanda, is this your husband?" John Carl wanted to know.

"Actually, John Carl, we're just engaged to be married, I told you that. We're not even married yet." That was music to John Carl's ears.

"Oh, Amanda, so this is what you've been doing on your off time?" he asked, now lashing out at her.

"Randall, don't cut into me. Our relationship has been over for a while, and you know that."

"Yeah, buddy, Amanda said what she had to say, so you can go now," John Carl threw in.

"Look, I don't care what you do, Amanda. I'm not here for your tired ass anyway. I'm here for my queen," he said, walking up to Ashley, grabbing her hand. She snatched her hand back so hard that she almost gave herself a hernia.

Uncle Jack and Uncle Jackson came strolling into the foyer, leaving Mr. and Mrs. Bell in the dining room all alone. They wanted to get in on the mess that had brewed between the Bell kids.

They didn't need to pull out all of their opening acts. The Bell kids were doing a bang up job of fucking up the holiday themselves. Now it was time to just sit back, watch, and tell John Carl "I told you so."

CHAPTER 25

911 Emergency

"Told you that shit was gone jump up and bite you in da ass, nephew," Jackson yelled into the air.

Uncle Jack, Aunt Dottie, and Aunt Beattie were ear hustling with front row seats.

"Uncle Jackson, not right now," John Carl countered.

Randall was still not budging. He had come there for Ashley, and before he left, he needed to profess his love. He hoped it would be enough for her to leave with him.

"Ashley, listen to me, baby. Can I please explain to you what's going on with Amanda and I?" Randall pleaded.

"Baby?" Mark repeated as he walked into the foyer, finally joining the household drama.

"You do understand that you're talking to my wife, right?" Mark asked Randall as he walked closer to him to get a good look directly into his eyes.

"Ashley, what the hell is he talking about? You better start telling me something and telling me something now."

"Aww shit! Erika, it's about to go down," Lance said, continuing to tape as he danced, holding the camera.

"Mark, listen. I don't want to talk about this right now," she said, brushing him off. "Randall, you need to take your ass home. I'm not dealing with you today. I can't even believe you would come over here. That is so disrespectful," Ashley finished.

"Did this dry head chap just say Randall was being disrespectful? This bamma done lost her whole entire mind. Girl, you running around throwing out pussy like you a contestant on the Housewives of LA. I know you ain't trying to talk about disrespect. You been sneaking around and disrespecting my brother all weekend," Lance spat back.

"Yep, Mark, Erika heard your sweet little wife here on the phone with Randall in the fitting room at the mall. Ask her where she went to get some air at last night."

"Don't ask me shit!" Asley yelled out. "I am so over everyone in this family. All y'all do is run y'all mouth. Talking about this one and talking about that one. Have you ever realized that not one of you are perfect?" she yelled out, giving a speech to everyone.

"Mark, just let me lay hands on this wench," Lance slid out with his bottom lip tucked. "Nancy Reagan here gone get her natural ass kicked today. I don't know who she think she talking to."

Erika got up from her seat slowly, walking in the direction of the commotion. Walking over slowly, she stood in front of Ashley and gave her a piece of her mind.

"Ashley, you know I barely even say anything, but I hear what goes on around here, and I see almost everything," Erika said, shifting to her left foot with her hand on her hip.

"I've watched you all weekend run circles around my brother. I've heard you on the phone with Randall many times over the last two days. Not one time have I seen you talk to or spend time with your husband or my nephew," she yelled into Ashley's face, making her point. "Have you ever noticed that my nephew has three hairs on his chin? Have you ever noticed that he spends more time on an electronic device than talking with his parents? Have you ever noticed that you just may be the problem in your household?" she continued to scold her sister-in-law. "Nah, I didn't think so," she said, getting a blank stare from Ashley.

"Look, I don't have time to listen to a speech from a half-wit, retarded virgin that still wears long johns under her pants in the winter. How about you get you a man, then you come talk to me about my relationship issues," she spat with fire to Erika.

"How about you be a mother and stop acting a whore off the Las Vega strip. And I might be a virgin, but at least I'm not jacking off to porn like your twelve-year old over there," Erika said pointing at Mark Jr. as he sat at the table sneaking on his cell phone that sat on his lap.

"Wait, what did you just say?" Mark asked.

"You heard me. Lance caught your son jacking off to porn. Now I don't have kids, excuse me if I'm wrong, but evidently, someone has not had the talk about the birds and the bees with that young man, now have they?" she asked. "So, again, I say to Mrs. Ashley stop being a whore and start being a mother, and don't come for my family! Ever!"

Everyone in the house was quiet. No one could even believe that Erika had clocked out and went the fuck off on Ashley.

Mr. and Mrs. Bell walked into the foyer slowly.

"Kids, listen," Mr. Bell started. "I been sitting in the other room listening to all this racket. You are grown men and women. You ought to be ashamed of yourselves, carrying on like this in front of these kids."

"Well, brother you know this one over here," Aunt Beattie said pointing at baby Poodah. "I don't know if you wanna call him a kid or a parasite," Aunt Beattie said as she and Dottie laughed.

"Beattie, shut the hell up!" he yelled. "I am so sick of this back and forth. This one hate that one. That one know something about this one's business. All y'all need to just grow the f—" he stopped mid-sentence.

Mr. Bell bent down to his knees, grabbing his chest. The pain he felt had knocked the wind out of his lungs. He could barely breathe and his heart was beating rather rapidly."

"Baby, are you okay?" Mrs. Bell cried out. "Oh Lord, somebody call 911 now. Dick, please, can you hear me?" she yelled on her knees, slapping his face softly.

"Dad, get up," Mark, Lance, Erika and Sharon cried out.

"Mr. Bell. Oh my God. Get up, please," Ashley said after the others.

Erika stood up and faced her with blood shot eyes. "Get your filthy tale out of my parents' house right now. All of this is your fault," she said while on the phone with the dispatch operator.

"Yes, ma'am, seven eighteen Greenbriar Road," she repeated her parents' address before hanging up the phone.

"The ambulance is on the way, Dad. Just hold on. We got you," Erika said, bending down to her father.

Mr. Bell had passed out on the floor but still had a pulse. Everyone in the house was frantic.

The baby had started crying, and Mrs. Bell had worry written all over her face.

Ashley had since grabbed her coat and purse and left, and so did Randall against his will.

Amanda decided to stay to comfort John Carl, and Erika wrapped her arms around their mother.

The ambulance arrived quickly, taking Mr. Bell's vitals and putting him on a gurney. Christmas dinner sat on the table getting cold while the whole family rushed to Greenville Hospital, praying that Mr. Bell was okay.

CHAPTER 26

FIX IT JESUS

The whole Bell family sat at Greenville Hospital for what seemed like forever. Babies were in the lobby crying, a hospital employee with a stuffy nose kept talking over the loud speaker, and the sound of sirens were etched in everyone's head.

John Carl and Mark's nerves were on edge.

Mr. Bell had been rushed back, and the doctor was working on him. After speaking with the EMS workers, they said that Mr. Bell had had a heart attack. They rushed him in as fast as they could.

Immediately, they set up for him to get an ultrasound of his heart, and if that didn't work, they would prepare for an MRI.

Mrs. Bell was worried. She didn't want them putting all that medication in Mr. Bell. Until now, he'd been as healthy as an ox. He was always going to walk around the block or at the mall. That was why everyone was so shocked that he would have a heart attack.

A nurse came out to the waiting area and called for the Bell family. Everyone stood from their seats, and Mark went over to help his mother out.

"We would like your family to follow me this way. We have a family room available that should fit your family while you wait."

Mrs. Bell turned to look at Mark. Her eyes held years of worry, and her hands shook like a leaf on a tree.

Mrs. Bell, Mark, Lance and David, John Carl and Amanda, Erika, Sharon and Gerald and their children all stood and followed the nurse's lead.

Once in the room, it was eerily quiet. No one wanted to talk. Most of them had a lump in their throats the size of a golf ball. The fear or Mr. Bell not making it was lingering in everyone's mind.

"Man, Momma, I'm so sorry," Mark spoke. "I completely apologize for my part in stressing Dad out. Had I not been standing there dealing with drama with my wife, this would not have happened."

"Markie, baby, that's nonsense. Listen, baby, we don't know what Daddy had going on. You know the man almost as old as Jesus, so you never know," she joked, trying to lighten the mood. "Mark, baby, listen, your daddy will be fine."

She looked around the room at the faces of all of her children who had, for the last two days, been at each other's heads.

There was even a moment when one had threatened to kill the other. But in moments like this were when they all knew to put the bull behind and stand by each other through thick and thin.

"All of you," Mrs. Bell continued, talking to her children. "Your dad will be just fine. He's a tough man, you guys know that. Besides, he's not going to leave here before getting all of his tools back that he's loaned Mark and John Carl."

Everyone burst out into laughter. They all knew that you could not borrow anything from their father without him writing it down.

He wrote down the date you got it, what it was, if it was scratched or damaged, when you said you would bring it back, and you had to sign it.

They all thought their father was over-possessive of his shit, but he was tired of not getting his things back.

As they all let their guards down with laughter, the nurse and the doctor were walking into the room.

Slowly, everyone's smile started to turn to a slight frown of worry.

"Hello, my name is Dr. Delvechio," he said, shaking Mrs. Bell's hand as she stood in front of all her children.

"Well, I want to say that I have good news and bad news. But Mr. Bell is okay for now."

A sigh of relief could be heard sliding through the room from everyone.

"Okay, doctor, so what's the bad news?" Mrs. Bell asked.

"Well, as it stands, we have stabilized his condition, but Mr. Bell has a clogged artery in his heart and we will need to do surgery soon to add a temporary stent. With your consent, we can get him on the list, and he should be having surgery in the next day or two. In the meantime, we'll keep him here in the hospital for full observation."

Mrs. Bell walked over to her chair slowly and sat down, resting her hand on her forehead, trying to think of another solution. She wanted to talk to Mr. Bell to see what he wanted to do.

"Momma, you gone sign the paper?" Sharon asked.

"I don't know, Sha Sha, I need to talk with your father. —Doctor, is he awake? Can I speak with him?"

"Well, he is under right now, but he's going in and out. He really needs to get some rest, but I will let you guys come in the room for just a moment."

They all grabbed their jackets and things and followed the doctor to the recovery room.

Mrs. Bell rushed to her husband's side, watching as his eyelids bounced up and down.

"Hello, daddy. It's me, your butterfly. I'm here with all of your crazy children. They're all still alive and they've all stopped arguing," she offered up.

As she talked, Mr. Bell squeezed her finger, letting her know that he could hear her.

"Oh, Lord, he grabbed my finger. Yes, Lord. Fix it, Jesus!" Mrs. Bell shouted.

"Momma," Sharon called out.

"What? Girl, don't call my name like this ain't a blessing. I will never be ashamed of calling on the Lord whenever and wherever I am. You betta get ahold of yourself, young lady," she told her daughter.

"Momma, I'm just saying. You're really loud."

"And you're really out of line. Now get out of your father's room with that mess, or get yourself together, Sharon Latriece Bell."

Sharon was embarrassed because she had gotten chastised in front of her siblings, and Mark was eating it all up.

"Told you, Kunta, one day that mouth was gone get your ugly ass in trouble," Mark said, making fun of her.

"Shut up, you uncircumcised reject," she threw back at her brother.

Mr. Bell's machines started to go off. His breathing had increased. His pressure was beginning to rise by the numbers on the machine.

Mrs. Bell rushed over and grabbed Sharon and Mark's arms at the same time. She dragged them both towards the door.

Once they were in the hall, Mrs. Bell turned to them with tear-filled eyes.

"Let me tell you two something. Your father is sick and tired of listening to all of you go at it like cats and dogs. It wouldn't surprise me if all your shenanigans ain't what stopped that man's heart. He just had a heart attack, and I'll be damned if he has another because you two can't keep your composure enough in public to act like the civilized human beings that we raised," she said, looking at her children as if they had lost their minds. "If you two can't stop the arguing, then you're going to have to go home. I'm not going to tolerate this nonsense in here at this hospital now. I'm just not," their mother demanded.

Sharon caught an attitude about the truth her mother told.

"You know what, you ain't gotta tell me twice. I have better things to do than sit up here and get yelled at because your grown son is acting like an infant."

"Sharon, what are you getting all hostile for? I was just joking with you."

"Well, there's a time and place for everything, and I ain't in no playing mood, so since everybody seems to be in their feelings," she said looking from her mother to her brother. "I'm going to get my worrisome family, and we will take our asses home. I'll come see my daddy on my own time. Don't bother stopping by my house or by Lace Fronts and Lashes. I'll talk to my daddy when I talk to my daddy."

With that, Sharon rushed into the room, calling out to Gerald and their kids. They all rushed into the hallway to leave.

Mrs. Bell sat there, flabbergasted at her daughter's outburst. She had no time to baby her grown ass daughter's feelings at the time. Mr. Bell was the one in need, and Sharon would just have to get over issues on her own.

CHAPTER 27

CATCH A CASE FOR MINE

Sharon was pissed when she left the hospital. Her blood was boiling she was perspiring from all ends.

She had made Gerald drive her to her parents' house so that she could get their bags and go home. Gerald sat in the car with the kids while she ran in to get their things.

Taking one last look at the dining room table, she noticed that Gerald's cell phone was sitting next to their baby's pacifier on the table. As she picked up the phone, it began to vibrate.

On quick display, it showed Big Booty Poochie.

Big Booty Poochie: *What's up big daddy. You gone come through and holler at me?*

Sharon took it upon herself to respond to see what she would get back.

Gerald/Sharon: *You know I will baby. Where you want me to come to?*

Big Booty Poochie: *Come to our normal spot. My mom house on Eastan dr.*

Gerald/Sharon: *What's the address again?*

Big Booty Poochie: *Boy I know you ain't forgot, you were just here two nights ago. 819 dang. Hurry up. I need to jump up on that.*

Gerald/Sharon: *(happy face emoji)*

Sharon was hot. Big Booty Poochie had just ended the great time they were having, living in their sexual hiatus. Sharon was ready to tear some shit up. She could not believe she had fallen for the shit that Gerald had fed her over the weekend.

She had slept with him, something she hadn't done since she found out how much he'd slept around on her.

Sharon was well known in the community for her beauty salon, and she also hosted a lot of community events for children.

Sharon had given so much time to Gerald, but constantly he cheated. She always found out one way or the other.

As Sharon walked to the car, Gerald could see the sour face Sharon had. There was no need for him to wonder what she was pissed off about now. At least a couple times a day she got pissed off at him for something.

Gerald popped the trunk, and Sharon threw their bags in the back and jumped back in the passenger seat.

Sharon didn't give herself time enough to close her door before going in on Gerald.

"So who the fuck is Big Booty Poochie?"

Gerald immediately started to hit at his pants pocket and his jacket pockets looking for his cell phone.

Sharon held his phone up so he could see she had it.

"See, the problem with you, Gerald, is that you don't even try to hide the shit. I am so sick of your cheating ass fucking with these hungry ass, misfit ass, disease filled, Snapchat, funky feet heffas then trying to lay up on me. I don't want to catch shit these li'l bitches might have given you. You can have that shit. I am so tired of your ass. Take me and my kids home. You can grab your shit and get the fuck out."

"Wait, hold up, Sharon. Let's talk about this."

"How about we not talk about this shit? Gerald, fuck you and the horse you rode in on. I'm done. I'm so sick of these females coming and showing they ass at my shop. The next bitch I have to bust in the head over you gone catch it, and you are too," she said with her voice full of anger.

"Sharon, can we just talk about this once we get home? I don't want to talk about this wit the kids in the car."

"Nigga, was you thinking about your kids when you was sticking your dick in other bitches? Don't think about them now!" Sharon yelled as Gerald pulled into their driveway. "Get your funky ass in here and get your shit and get out my house. Big Booty Poochie said you can come over her momma house on Eastan. Go layup with them hoes," Sharon said, slamming the car door before walking towards the house.

Gerald sat in the car for a moment, trying to figure out what his next move would be.

Their baby was in the back seat crying up a storm, and Cammy was calling her daddy's name over and over again.

Gerald's head was full.

Between all the drama at Sharon's parents' house with her siblings, to her father being in the hospital, he didn't know if he was coming or going.

Gerald took the kids in the house. He went back outside to get their bags to bring them into the house.

Once he was done, Sharon was standing in the kitchen, drinking some juice, looking out the kitchen window.

"Sharon, I don't want them other women, baby. Please, can we just talk about this?" Gerald asked.

"Gerald, we don't have shit to talk about."

Just then, Gerald's phone began to vibrate in Sharon's hand again.

Quickly, she answered when she saw it was Poochie again.

"What up?" she grunted into the phone.

"Can I speak to Gerald?"

"Bitch, no you can't speak to my babies' father. I'm gone ask your ass to get a life and your own man."

"Why the fuck is you answering his phone? Oh, you must be in your feelings, Mrs. Beauty shop girl. Well, check this out, Gerald been filling this pussy up for a while, so it seems like I ain't the one you need to be having a beef with."

"Bitch, please. I'll tell you what, since you got all the mouth in the world come holla at me hoe."

"Come holla at you for what? Your man still gone be fuckin' other bitches. I don't understand what the fuck you getting all hostile for."

"Oh, bitch. I got your hostile. I'm beating your ass on sight, soon as I see you."

"Hoe, run up. I guarantee you getting both your eyes shut."

"Bet. I got you, bitch," Sharon yelled as she hit the button to disconnect the call.

She threw Gerald's phone clear across the room. It landed right upside his head, leaving a hickey on his forehead.

"Sharon, stop it!" Gerald yelled after her.

She walked through their home, yelling and cursing. Every word that was made to be profanity, she used in a matter of seconds.

"Sorry, muthafucka," she said out loud to herself as she put their things away in their bedroom.

Gerald walked into the room and shut the door after getting the kids down for a nap as Sharon continued to fuss.

Gerald walked behind her, grabbing a big chunk of her ass into his hands.

"Sharon, I know you're upset, baby, but please don't make me leave. I don't want to be without you and my kids," he said as he tried to continue to feel her up from behind.

She closed her eyes, upset and frustrated, but his touch felt good as hell.

"Gerald, I can't deal with your shit. I'm exhausted. I'm tired. I'm just plain tired of it. Stop touching me."

"Sharon, listen to me—"

She pulled away quickly, trying to get Gerald's hands from being planted on her ass.

"I know you don't think you getting no pussy now, do you?"

"Sharon," he said, giving her the puppy eyes.

He grabbed her hips again, rubbing his penis on her ass through their clothes.

"Gerald, get your shit."

"But, Sharon, listen. Can we talk, baby?" he asked, turning her around to face him.

It took everything in her to stop herself from looking into his eyes. It only took a matter of seconds, and she was hooked.

The look that Gerald had given her made her insides melt. She knew her nigga wasn't shit, but she loved his ass.

Gerald picked Sharon up. By instinct, she threw her legs around his waist.

Softly, he laid her body on the bed while sliding his hand underneath her shirt. Gerald slowly popped button after button from her shirt as she squirmed.

Softly, he delivered licks and kisses to her neck. The rush of the sensation she felt in her body was unfathomable.

Gerald had done his homework. He'd been laying down all the stops. Whenever she came close to letting him get the pussy, he was going to go completely overboard just to stay on the roster as the fiancé another day.

Their breathing began to increase. Their motions got wilder and their grinding got harder. He stuck his hand into her pants while looking in her eyes. Without warning, his fingers entered her wetness.

Sharon closed her eyes, letting her soul accept every inch of love it was being given.

As Gerald seductively rocked her pussy, he sucked her bottom lip. Her eyes rolled in her head while his fingers rolled in her pussy.

Gerald wanted to make sure Sharon had forgotten about the whole phone call, and he wasn't convinced he had made it to that point yet.

His body crept backwards on the bed with his tongue leaving a trail down her torso.

Still manipulating her dripping wetness, slowly, he wrapped his lips around her clitoris.

His tongue was like a python that had been let loose. Sharon's pussy pulsated.

It throbbed... It grew... As he sucked, she moaned. As he grunted, she screamed. When he stuck himself inside of her harder, she came long and strong, releasing an orgasm that would stop the masses.

Gerald and Sharon fell back onto the bed, satisfied and sexed up. Sharon knew she was going around and around on an emotional rollercoaster with Gerald, but she loved his cheating ass and just couldn't let him go.

She'd be damned if he got caught being seen with someone else. All hell would break loose, so for now, she was going to forgive but not forget.

Sharon got up from the bed and walked into the bathroom to shower. Once she came out, Gerald was just getting up from his intermission.

"Baby, are you hungry?" Sharon asked with a coo.

"Yeah, baby, I am. I was thinking steak and eggs," he returned in a boss voice.

"Okay, baby, I got you. You relax. Momma gone get you right," she cooed again in her "baby you fucked the shit out of me" voice.

That's what that good dick do for you, Sharon thought as she walked to the kitchen. I will body a bitch about Gerald's ass. Let a bitch walk up in Lace Fronts and Lashes if she wants to. I will catch a case for that one, she continued to think to herself with a brow in the air as she prepared to cook for her fiancé.

Hopefully, Gerald had learned his lesson, but time would tell.

CHAPTER 28

LOVE ME OR LEAVE ME ALONE

It had been two days and the whole family was still at the hospital with Mr. Bell. Everyone except Sharon.

Sharon was still in her feelings from her and Mark being checked by their mother about their disrespectful mouths. She hadn't been up to the hospital because she wasn't one to apologize. She knew at some point, she was going to have to apologize at least to her mother, but that time hadn't come for her yet. So, in the meantime, Sharon was being her stubborn old self. She wasn't communicating with anyone in the family. She went back to business at the shop. Head first busy every day as usual until New Years.

She hadn't had any more problems out of Gerald or his mistress' calls.

Back at the hospital, tension rose the moment Ashley walked into the building to check on her father-in-law.

Somehow, she'd gotten the notion in her head that everyone would forgive her for cheating on Mark. Her little hiatus for a couple of days just may have not been enough.

"Hey, Mark," she whispered, walking into Mr. Bell's hospital room.

"Ashley, what are you doing here? You're not welcome here," Mark shot back boldly.

"Mark, please, I know you're very upset with me right now, and I get that. But that does not negate the fact that I'm still your wife, and I love your parents. We have a lot of shit to work out. I get that, but I'm not going to let the shit between us fuck up my relationship with everyone else," she said, trying to convince Mark that she was serious.

"Whatever, Ashley. You can twist your speech any way you choose fit. Me and my son are just fine without you sleeping around town with people."

Sharon's eyes got big, and Mrs. Bell gasped for air, and Mark Jr's lips got as white as a powder house. He thought he was hearing things. That last statement threw everyone for a loop.

Lance sat in the corner with Erika, eating chips and waiting for the rest of the tea to spill.

"You know what, Mark, I can't talk to you right now," she said, looking around the room at the rest of the family. Everyone was waiting for her to say something to defend the allegations.

Ashley decided to do just the opposite. She was tired of explaining herself. She was tired of trying to prove herself to the family that had taken her in. The cat had been let out the bag. There was nothing she could do to take it back. Mark would never forgive her.

"Mark, I'm going to go to the airport and get a rental car. I'll drive home alone, and I would expect for us to talk when you and Mark Jr. arrive," she demanded.

Mark turned, putting his back to her as if he hadn't heard a word she said.

As she turned to walk out of the room, she thought Randall would take her even if she had on dirty draws. He was so desperate to have her be his. That still did not negate the fact that he had a whole fiancée that he hadn't even told her about.

Ashley's next task was to talk to Randall to see just what in the hell was on his mind. Why hadn't he told her that he was engaged? Most importantly, why the hell he felt it was okay for him to come to her in-laws' house trying to be captain save a hoe?

Amanda was still right by John Carl's side. She didn't care what Randall was doing. She had long gotten over their relationship anyway. John Carl was just her saving grace. He made her feel okay with doing what she wanted, especially with Randall living in Georgia.

She did love Randall. She did want to marry him, but they had just grown apart. The love was not what it used to be, and it seemed as if they were forcing their relationship. It had been months since they had slept together. The feelings just were not there.

As fast as Amanda was moving with John Carl, you'd think that relationship would be a bust as well. But as it stood, John Carl seemed to be toting Amanda around everywhere that he went. Just as the family had not left the hospital with Mr. Bell, neither had she.

It was as if she were glued to John Carl's hip and he'd have to pry her clingy ass off. John Carl had Amanda in serious lust, and she didn't want to lose that feeling.

John Carl, on the other hand, was content with her beauty and her expedited attraction to him. He liked her just the same. New for him to be into a woman mentally and physically and really mean it. But this time, John Carl seemed to be serious.

He'd decided to give him and Amanda a shot.

He wasn't worried about Randall at all. He knew the way he'd mind fucked Amanda, she would be on his roster with or without Randall's blessing. Deciding to just go with the union, they decided to stick around each other to see where life would take them.

CHAPTER 29

JUST IN TIME FOR NEW YEAR'S

Mr. Bell was finally released from the hospital. He and Mrs. Bell had settled back into their home after his long stay in the hospital. They were glad the surgery had been a success. The stent had been put in, and Mr. Bell's heart was beating just as strong as a teenage running track.

Lance and Erika kept up with their house while they were not there. The night of the incident, they went back to the house and put the food away and cleaned the dining room and kitchen.

A few days later, they had to go right back and throw everything out since no one was there to eat all of the leftovers.

Mr. Bell had been quiet since he'd been released from the hospital. Mrs. Bell tried to bring up topic after topic to get him to speak. He just wasn't in the mood. His heart was still full from all the commotion that was going on before he was rushed to the ER.

He hated for his children to fight. He hated for them to be at odds.

Mrs. Bell went into the kitchen and prepared a nice pot of homemade chicken noodle soup for Mr. Bell after he got settled.

Mr. Bell laid back in his bed, grabbed his cell phone, and put together a group text including all of his children. None of them had come over to the house since they made it.

Mark and Mark Jr. hadn't even left. They were staying at Mr. and Mrs. Bell's still. They just weren't there when they arrived.

Mr. Bell: *Hey kids, it's ya daddy. Me and your momma at the house. I'm gonna get some rest tonight but I want each and every one of you here at my house tomorrow at five o'clock in the evening. No exceptions. Everyone better be present. And everyone better bring better attitudes.*

With that, he ended his group text. His phone beeped over and over getting responses from his children confirming that they would be there. The only one he didn't get a response from was Sharon.

Mrs. Bell had filled him in on the dynamics of her anger. He wanted to go over to her house to talk to her, but Mrs. Bell wouldn't hear of it.

Mr. Bell sent out another text message. This time, just to Sharon.

Mr. Bell: *Hey Shan Shan. It's ya daddy baby. Just wanted to let you know they let a old man out that hospital. I wanna see you love bug. Drop on by the house tomorrow at 5. I know you ain't answering nobody else, but if you don't answer me I will come to your house little girl.*

Mr. Bell knew that if anyone could get through to Sharon, it would be him. Sharon had somehow gotten the bad end of the stick when it came to people picking sides. She was a daddy's girl. She and Mrs. Bell always seemed to be at odds, but her saving grace was her father. He was always choosing the side with Sharon and demanded everyone leave her alone.

That was the biggest reason she spazzed out at the hospital.

Knowing her father was lying in the hospital bed not able to speak or move or talk to them had taken a toll on her.

Sharon got both of her father's messages and text him back quickly.

Sharon: *Hi daddy. I got both of your messages. I will be there daddy but could you please tell your son Mark to keep his comments to his self?*

Mr. Bell: *Yes Shan Shan, don't worry about Mark. See you tomorrow.*

With that, he ended their correspondence, setting his phone back on the night stand. For the rest of the night, he rested up, and Mrs. Bell ran to the grocery store to get food for the following day.

Mr. Bell had had enough of his kids' shit. He was going to get them together once and for all.

CHAPTER 30

GET THAT ACT RIGHT

The following day had come and gone. Mrs. Bell had baked homemade red velvet cake cookies and homemade frosting for her kids and a peach cobbler for Mr. Bell. She had about ten minutes, and all the kids would be showing up.

As she went to set the cookies on the table, she could see Lance and Erika pulling into the driveway. She shifted back to the kitchen to grab a roll of paper towels and paper plates to set on the table. Mark and Mark Jr. were pulling in just about the same time as John Carl.

Slowly, everyone filed into the house gathering in the dining room to grab cookies and a cup of milk that was prepared.

Sharon was the last of the Mohicans. She hadn't showed up yet. It was a Thursday evening, and she was busy at Lace Fronts and Lashes. She'd tried to slow her schedule, but due to the holiday, there was just no way she could get away.

Mr. Bell had come down from his bedroom. Comfortably, he sat in his black leather La-Z Boy diagonal from his seventy-inch flat screen. Patiently, he waited for his kids to mingle with each other while waiting for Sharon to arrive.

Mrs. Bell was talking with Lance as they all walked into the room to sit with Mr. Bell. Lance pulled out his cell and dialed up Sharon one more time.

Since she didn't answer again, he decided to leave her another message. "Sharon where are you? We at Momma and Daddy house waiting on you, girl. Hurry up. —Daddy, your light skin daughter playing games right now," he said as Erika snickered.

"Hey, now. That's what we're here for, Lance. Since you wanna start in on your sister, I guess I'll go ahead and get started. I'll just fill your sister in later when she decides to call one of us back. Did anyone try calling Gerald?" Mr. Bell asked.

Erika and Lance looked at each other, shaking their heads no. John Carl and Mark did the same.

"Okay, well, listen. After what happened at Christmas dinner, you all know now that me and your mother won't be here forever."

"You better speak for yourself," Mrs. Bell joked as they all laughed.

"Well, anyway, I guess your mother must have some type of bubble she gone live in that's gone keep her alive forever," he came back with.

"Listen, I want you guys to know that I love you all very much. Having that heart attack really got an old man thinking. The way you all were acting at that Christmas dinner was just despicable. I don't mean that lightly. I mean everything that could have happened in this family happened that day," he continued to say, looking around the room at his children.

"But, Dad, to be honest, all that was Mark and his wife's fault. Nobody else had anything to do with all the drama that was going on," John Carl blurted out.

"John Carl, you spare me your belly aching. You are just as much to blame as Mark and his wife. Listen, I feel like I'm on a bad episode of Jerry Springer. You're screwing with a woman that's engaged, and her fiancé is sleeping with your brother's wife. You have absolutely no room to pass judgement on anyone," Mr. Bell continued on.

He got up from his seat slowly, and Mrs. Bell rushed over to him to secure him if he were to fall.

He held out his hand for her to stand back. He raised himself from the chair and held on to the arm of the couch as he spoke to his kids.

"Listen, kids. The moral of this meeting is to remind you all that we're family. Your mother and I didn't raise you all to be running around arguing and fighting with each other. We raised you to have dignity. To respect one another. To always cherish family. If you don't have anyone on earth, you have God, and you have your family. I want you kids to start acting like it. The way you all were acting was unacceptable, and I had better not ever see you all acting that way again. Everybody is going to make up. Everybody is going to get along, and that's all I have to say about that," he said, turning to his oldest son.

"Mark, I don't even know what to say to you, man. You got a bad situation going on," Mr. Bell said to his son, disappointed. "I guess all I can say is use your judgment. If you love Ashley, then you'll forgive her and you'll work this thing out."

Mark stood to the side looking stupid. He was so confused. He was still in a daze, he couldn't believe Ashley had been having an affair all that time. Not one time did he ever think that she would betray their love the way that she had. That was one thing that Mark didn't think he would ever be able to forgive. He loved Ashley to death, but for her to give her body to another was the ultimate for Mark. At some point, he had to stand for something. Infidelity just was not a trait he was willing to adapt to.

CHAPTER 31

DON'T FUCK WITH YOUR EYES CLOSED

It hadn't even been a full week, and Gerald was on Sharon's shit list once again. Sharon needed to leave the shop to go to a meeting at her parents' house. Gerald had dropped Sharon off at Lace Fronts and Lashes that morning and was supposed to pick her up at four forty-five. Even though she wasn't done with her last client, Gerald still hadn't showed. Their kids were at the daycare center, and he was supposed to pick them up at three. She'd called his cell at least five times and got no answer.

After calling the daycare center, finding out that her children were still there, she began to get worried. She hoped that nothing had happened to him.

Sharon asked one of the other stylists, Koo Koo, to give her a ride to the daycare and to her house.

Koo Koo put her client under the dryer, grabbed her keys and purse, and they headed out.

When Sharon got to the daycare center, it was about five fifteen. There were only four kids left to be picked up. Her and Gerald's two and two others. Two of the girls that worked in the daycare were sitting over to the side looking at Sharon, snickering. She walked past them, and it warranted a laugh each time. She knew the shit was a little different, but she didn't want to make a scene.

Sharon threw her babies' car seats over her left arm, and she grabbed Cammy's hand. As she walked to the door, the two workers broke out in laughter again.

Sharon knew there were three young, Pop Tart bitches that worked in the daycare, but she never paid them any mind.

"Is it something y'all leaving me out on? What's so damn funny?" Sharon stopped and asked with a smirk on her face.

"Girl, bye, ain't nobody laughing at you," the girl with the horrible lace front said.

"Ain't you engaged to Gerald?" the other asked.

"Yes, I am. And?" Sharon asked, shifting her baby a little lower to the ground in case she needed to leap on a bitch.

"Mmm... Nothing, boo. You ain't gotta get all up in arms. I was just wondering. Yo car cute, though. Don't you got a Dodge Challenger?" the messy twenty-year old asked.

"Look, why all the questions? You know something I don't? Just let that shit out. What the fuck is it?" Sharon asked. Now she was pissed. Her earlier feeling about Gerald being hurt had long left her mind.

With all the questioning, now she felt like Gerald's ass was doing something he didn't have any fucking business doing, and these bitches knew just what it was.

Sharon decided to leave well enough alone. She stormed out of the daycare with her kids in tow.

She buckled her kids in the back seat of Koo Koo's car, and they were headed to Sharon's house.

Sharon pulled out her cell during the ride and saw she had a few phone calls from Lance. After listening to his messages, she knew there was no need for her to head over there after getting her car.

As they pulled on her street, she could see her car was parked in the driveway, and there was a Kia Optima parked at the curb in the front.

"Koo Koo, stay right here with my kids for a second. If it's a bitch in my house, I'm blowing this muthafucka up!" she grunted through gritted teeth.

Sharon walked to the door calmly. Her right jean pocket held her mace, and her right hand held her keys.

She walked into the house quietly and walked into each room until she got into the bathroom off from the kitchen.

There he was. Gerald's beige ass standing in the bathroom with his head in the air facing the ceiling, enjoying the fruits of a dirty thot sucking his dick into an orgasm.

Before Gerald could think straight, he was being hit in the mouth.

When Sharon got in arms' reach, she straddled the bitch on the floor from behind and hit Gerald in his face so hard, it dazed him.

"Ahhhh!" the girl screamed, trying to scramble to get up from the floor.

Sharon's legs were on each side of her, so there wasn't far she could go. Gerald had bent down towards the floor to wipe the dripping blood from his lip. Sharon had hit his ass with every ounce of anger she had in her soul.

"Bitch, I cannot believe you got this hoe in my house!" she screamed, still swinging at his head.

The female Gerald had slobbing him down had slid her way out of Sharon's grasp. Once out into the kitchen, she tried to break and run for it.

Sharon was not letting that happen, and the bitch was in her house. She could give her a thot pass for sucking Gerald's little nasty dick, but coming in another female's house was the ultimate "get your ass beat" rule.

She grabbed the back of the girl's wig, yanking her body right back to where she was. She beat the girl in the head for old and new and talked to her.

"Bitch, this gone be your one and only fuckin' time coming up in another bitch house to fuck they nigga!" she yelled as she delivered blow after blow to the girl's eye.

Out of nowhere, she realized the bitch she was wailing on was the third bitch from the daycare center.

Sharon's screams got louder as she turned from the girl and back to Gerald.

"The bitch from the damn daycare center, Gerald?" she cried out. "What the fuck is wrong with you, man?"

The daycare worker was horrified. She didn't know whether to move or be still. She hopped up off the floor as soon as Sharon turned around. The girl's reflexes prompted her to grab a knife that was sitting on the edge of the sink.

Just as Sharon launched at her, the knife went deep into Sharon's flesh.

Gerald let out a loud, guttural cry. "Sharon! No! Bitch, what did you do?"

Cries rang out from Sharon and Gerald simultaneously. The sorrow mixed in their cries made for a sad horrifying situation.

"I'm sorry. I didn't mean to hurt her. I gotta go. I gotta leave."

Gerald stood, grabbing the girl around the neck. Her eye leaked from the beating she'd received from Sharon.

In the meantime, Sharon laid on the ground, crying and moaning from the pain.

"Bitch, your ass ain't going no fuckin' where," he said, holding her with the left hand as he called 911 on his cell with the right.

After he got off with EMS, he placed a call to Lance.

"Well, it's about time either you or Sharon called somebody," Lance said sarcastically.

"Lance, listen to me. Something's wrong with Sharon."

"Boy, y'all fighting again?"

"Lance, listen to me. Sharon got stabbed. EMS is on their way to our house. Meet us at the hospital."

Lance turned and looked at the phone that he held. The family was looking at the look on his face, wondering what the shock was for.

"That was Gerald," he said. "He said Sharon got stabbed and she's on her way to the hospital. He doesn't know her condition, and he didn't say who stabbed her."

Mr. Bell grabbed his chest, and so did Mrs. Bell.

Mark rushed over to grab their mother from falling. Everyone grabbed their things and headed out of the house as fast as they could.

Fifteen minutes later, they had made it to the hospital. The only thing that they had been told was that they were trying to stabilize her condition.

Mrs. Bell went down to the chapel while they waited.

She bent to her knees and went to the most high for healing.

"Father God, please wrap your arms around my baby. For I know not the circumstances, you are an awesome healer. You are our provider. You are the conqueror of all. Father God, please cover my child in your blood. Heal her, Father God," she prayed and cried.

As Mrs. Bell got up from her knees, Mr. Bell was walking through the door. The look on his face was horrified. It was as if he'd seen a ghost. His look left worry all over Mrs. Bell's face.

"Richard, what is it?"

"Sit down, Regina."

"No. What is wrong with my baby?" she cried, walking closer to her husband. "What is wrong with my baby?" she continued to cry.

Mr. Bell grabbed her close. He wrapped his arms around the love of his life and the mother of his children. His heart ached to see her in such pain.

He just couldn't bring himself to tell her what he came to tell her. Instead, he sat with his wife on one of the pews and held her close as they prayed together for the saving grace of their family. The family that they had begun to build over thirty years ago.

There was not one trial or tribulation that the Bells had not been able to conquer. Their belief was that God would never let them down.

But at this moment in the Bells' life, they were wondering if God had forgotten about them.

THE END...to be continued...

Up Next for Author S.
Chameleon....

COMING SOON......

"Lace Fronts and Lashes"

Gerald and Sharon's story

"Lace Fronts and Lashes"

CHAPTER 1

"What you do in the dark"

COMING SOON

Chameleon Publications

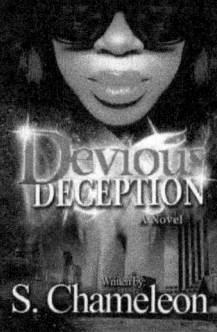

NENE CAPRI PRESENTS
Devious DECEPTION
A Novel
Written By S. Chameleon

NENE CAPRI PRESENTS
Devious DECEPTION II
S. Chameleon
Author Of Real Soldiers Don't Die

CHAMELEON PUBLICATIONS Presents
REAL SOLDIERS DON'T DIE
S. Chameleon

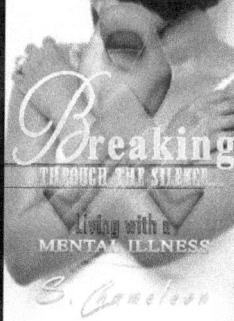

CHAMELEON PUBLICATIONS
Breaking THROUGH THE SILENCE
Living with a MENTAL ILLNESS
S. Chameleon

COMING SOON!

Chameleon Cosmetics

Products will include Lip Gloss, Lip Stick,

Eyeshadow,

Eyebrow Definer, Concealer, Foundation, Eye

lashes and

Much more.

To become a distributor for Chameleon

Cosmetics please email S.Chameleon

chameleonpublications@gmail.com

Author Bio

Author S. Chameleon has always been a "BOSS". The full-time wife and mother of two has never taken her writing talent for granted. The Author originated from Saginaw, Michigan, she then moved to Grand Rapids, Michigan and she continued to flourish. From her many carriers to her personality, she's always has had a style all of her own and reigns supreme as she unleashes her many fictional personalities in her writing.

Chameleon is an author with NeNe Capri Presents and has released two Novels under that imprint. S. Chameleon is also the C.E.O. of Chameleon Publications. She has released three Novels and one book under her independent imprint to date. The Author is not only a writer of street literature. As a Chameleon would change and adapt to its habitat, you'll see that in the Authors up and coming Novels as well. In the coming months the Author will be delivering Suspense, Thriller, Drama, Love and Erotica.

The Author also has a children book series and teen book series that will be releasing in the near future as well as a Cosmetics line Deva' by: Samantha Jax so make sure you keep an eye out for that.
For all her fellow Chameleons readers and followers of her blog, here is what you've been waiting for! So stay connected, It's only up from here baby.

"Act Like A Lady Think Like A BOSS"
www.schameleonbooks.blogspot.com
IG &Twitter&Periscope: SChameleon_1
FB: Author SChameleon
LinkedIn: Author Schameleon

9780692821886